What Page, Sir?

SIMON PICKERING

What Page, Sir?

Red Door

Published by RedDoor
www.reddoorpress.co.uk

The author and publisher gratefully acknowledge permissions granted to reproduce the copyright material in this book.

p. 3, 4, 6, 7, 11, 12, 13 © *Lord of the Flies* by William Golding, published by Faber and Faber Ltd. Reproduced with kind permission.

p. 3, 4, 6, 7, 11, 12, 13 © *Lord of the Flies* by William Golding, published by The Random House Group Ltd. Reproduced with kind permission.

p.14, 15, 19, 20, 21, 22 from *The Inspector Calls and Other Plays* by J. B. Priestly published by The Random House Group Ltd. An Inspector Calls copyright 1947 by J. B. Priestly. Reproduced by permission of The Random House Group Ltd.

p. 33, 34 from *The Old Man and The Sea* by Ernest Hemingway published by The Random House Group Ltd. © Hemingway Foreign Rights Trust 1952. Reproduced by permission of The Random House Group Ltd.

p. 33, 34 from *The Old Man and the Sea* by Ernest Hemingway. Copyright 1952 by Ernest Hemingway. Copyright renewed 1980 by Mary Hemingway. Reprinted with the permission of Scribner, a division of Simon & Schuster, Inc. All rights reserved.

p. 53, 82 from *A Handful of Dust* by Evelyn Waugh published by Penguin Books Ltd. © Copyright 1934 by Evelyn Waugh. Reproduced by permission of Penguin Books Ltd. ©

p. 65, 66, 67, 68, 69, 70, 71, 72 from *Journey's End* by R. C. Sherriff published by Penguin Classics. Copyright © 1929 by R. C. Sheriff. Reprinted by permission of The Random House Group Limited.

p. 25, 79, 80 from *Decline and Fall* by Evelyn Waugh published by Penguin Books Ltd. © Copyright 1928 by Evelyn Waugh. Reproduced by permission of Penguin Books Ltd. ©

p.76, 77 from Brighton Rock by Graham Greene, published by The Random House Group Ltd. Reproduced with permission of David Higham Associates.

Every effort has been made to trace the copyright holders and obtain permission to reproduce this material. The publisher apologises for any errors or omissions in the above list and would be grateful if notified of any corrections that should be incorporated in future reprints or editions of this book.

ISBN 978-1-913062-69-9

A CIP catalogue record for this book is available from the British Library

Cover design: Sarah Whittaker

Printed and bound in Denmark by Nørhaven

For the Mole

Contents

Introduction

For English teachers the English Literature GCSE exams have often been the occasion of their annual meltdown or grand strop. It used to be brought on by pupils who forgot their set texts, apparently oblivious to the advantage of using their own copies containing all the notes and annotations they'd made throughout the course. More recently, it was sweating over whether there were enough clean copies of the exam texts, and sometimes having to resort to frantically rubbing out their annotations.

But that's now a thing of the past since the two papers became 'closed book' exams – effectively taking the English literature out of the English Literature exam. Without books to worry about, the main concern now is what questions the exam board has set. After all the work your students might have done on texts like *Macbeth* or *Great Expectations* or *Animal Farm*, they will be given a choice of just two questions on their Modern Text, and no choice at all for Shakespeare and the Nineteenth-Century Novel. Obviously, the idea is to prepare them to be able to cope with whatever comes up in the exam paper, but it isn't always possible to anticipate the exam board's next move. A few years ago, I recall feeling extremely indignant with our exam board for setting the character-based question for *Pride and Prejudice* on Lydia Bennet, a relatively minor character, who, needless to say, I had not got round to looking at properly. Now there are Student Chat Rooms, which devote considerable time and nervous energy to discussing various doomsday scenarios, such as what one should do in the event of *An Inspector Calls* question on Edna, the maid.

It can also be hard to anticipate how your students will react to the pressure cooker of the exam room. On one occasion, in the GCSE English Literature exam, I challenged a boy in my class, who I had spotted answering on a text that we hadn't read or studied. 'This one looks easier, sir,' he replied.

It wasn't the time or place to argue with him, so feeling a mixture of resignation and professional despair, I went back to invigilating – the slow walk, up and down the rows of bowed heads in the sports hall. Over one boy's shoulder, etched into the varnished surface of his desk – in amongst the usual X-rated graffiti about other pupils and members of staff – was another discouraging message: 'Poetry is gay'.

This, or groaning, is often the response of pupils towards poetry. In one lesson as I attempted to move on from *Pride and Prejudice* to the obligatory exam board poetry anthology, somebody muttered, 'What's this shit?' as soon as they realised that the book on their desk contained poetry. One of the few advantages of the coronavirus for teenagers might be that they don't have to sit an exam on poetry this year. But most of the old favourites – *An Inspector Calls*, *Romeo and Juliet*, *Lord of the Flies*, *A Christmas Carol*, *Macbeth*, and the rest – will still be there for teenagers next summer, and probably beyond, regardless of the global pandemic, and whatever might follow it, or the preferences of English teachers and their pupils.

Not being on the same page/wavelength as your students is an occupational hazard for all teachers, and one that you seem to experience more acutely the older you get. But for English teachers, as well as the metaphorical divide between you and the pupils, there's also the nuts and bolts challenge of everyone in the class finding the right page in the book you are supposed to be reading. And this is just where the joy of text in the secondary school classroom begins...

Chapter One

Lord of the Flies

A few weeks ago, on my fifty-third birthday, I accepted what will be my third maternity cover (temporary Teacher of English post) in the last two years. There was a strong smell of manure blowing across the staff car park as I returned to my car and, for a few moments, sat staring despondently into space before driving away, back to the safety of the half-term holiday.

That was at the end of May, in the tenth week of the first coronavirus lockdown. In February I had applied for a job at this school, but didn't get as far as an interview; now I have been offered a job without any formal interview because they are desperate, after an English teacher resigned at the eleventh hour – i.e. on the last day before half-term. Presumably, the pool of Newly Qualified Teachers has dried up this late in the day. Like Stella Artois, in teaching terms I am comparatively, or rather 'reassuringly', expensive (code for old), but the head teacher has no choice but to take me on.

There was still a strong whiff of the countryside

when I visited the school a few weeks later to pick up my timetable, be given log-in details, and meet the Head of Department. One of the deflating bits of information they shared with me was that I would be starting the school year with *Lord of the Flies* by William Golding. I consoled myself that I have at least read it and taught it before, and quite recently – to Year 10 girls at the independent school where I filled in, just before and during lockdown, for another temporary teacher. She, like me, had failed to get the permanent position back in February, took umbrage it seems, and disappeared.

I have been here before. Not just in March at the posh girls' school, but twenty-seven years ago with the Year 10 class I was given on Teaching Practice as a student teacher. The school was in Eastwood, an old mining town a few miles north of Nottingham, and the birthplace of D H Lawrence. I was to devote the whole of the spring term to *Lord of the Flies*, the frosty female Head of Department explained.

My old English Teacher, Mr Tooth, had tried to interest our class in the novel at some point during the third year – Year 9. The names Piggy and Ralph seemed familiar but nothing else remained through the fog of those lessons. Ralph's name, in particular, was memorable because of Mr Tooth's strangely clipped way of saying it, but that was about it. A second reading over the Christmas holidays was definitely required before I could start teaching it.

For readers who haven't read *Lord of the Flies*, or seen the film, it is set during or possibly after World War Two, on an unspecified Pacific-style island, where a plane carrying a group of English schoolboys crashes amongst the creepers and palm trees. It is a miraculously soft landing for the boys who spend Chapter One emerging from the broken plane and the jungle on to the beach, somewhat disorientated but apparently unharmed. Only the pilot and adult chaperones don't make it. For teenage readers, who tend to value realism and adopt a literal stance towards fiction, the opening prompts a number of difficult questions: why are there no adults still standing who could organise things properly; why are these boys being evacuated by plane in the tropics instead of by train to Wales and the south-west like everyone else; and why are some of them travelling long haul dressed as choristers, even if they are members of the choir?

The head chorister, Jack Merridew, misses out in the vote to be chief to 'the fair boy'/golden boy, Ralph, who finds the all-important conch in Chapter One. Daddy, somewhat predictably, is a naval commander, and will come and rescue them, Ralph boasts, as soon as he has a spot of leave. Despite his working-class background, and being described by Ralph at the moment of discovery as an 'irrelevance', it is Piggy who has seen a conch before, and knows what it is and that it can be blown like a bugle. But because of

Piggy's asthma (referred to plummily by Ralph as 'ass-mar') it is left to Ralph to sound the horn and summon the other boys out of the jungle for their first meeting. Jack has to make do with being in charge of the choir, who on his command remove their cloaks ('All right choir. Take off your togs') and become the hunters. The battle lines and neat thematic divide visible at this first bad-tempered meeting – the values of civilisation and democracy (Piggy, Ralph and the conch) versus barbarism and dictatorship (Jack and the choir) – then play out through more than two hundred pages of densely obscure description and stilted dialogue. The other divide is between Piggy, and everyone else, who appear to have come from public schools.

Worryingly, the question which nagged away at me during that first reading over Christmas in 1992 – what was I supposed to do with it – hasn't become much clearer with time and experience. The Head of Department in my first teaching job offered very solid advice in relation to teaching novels and plays to secondary school pupils: deliver the story first, and don't try to be too clever. You, the teacher, might know who's who in the text and what happens in what order but most of them won't. A simpler and more appealing alternative to *Lord of the Flies* from the list of so-called Modern Texts is *An Inspector Calls*. It is generally regarded as a straightforward play, actually a bit too obvious for a GCSE exam text, but this hasn't always proved to be the case. Before I could take one particularly difficult group anywhere near the play's themes – the Inspector's message of social responsibility and so on – I had a desperate struggle just to establish the various identities of the characters at the start of the play: a family of four, plus one guest. It is best not to take anything for granted.

At least with *An Inspector Calls*, reading the play together is a good way to start things off, but reading just a couple of pages from *Lord of the Flies* out loud to a class is likely to send them to sleep. Another approach is to ask members of the class to read the character parts as if it were a play, whilst the teacher reads/edits/skips the long passages of description. But this also runs into trouble with *Lord of the Flies* – partly because the speaker is often not clearly identified, and also because what fragments of dialogue the characters are given never seem to justify the breathless urgency of the narrative and all the exclamation marks. In Chapter Two, for example, a section of apparently trivial conversation about making a bonfire is, according to the narrative, rather more than it seems. Ralph, inexplicably, goes red in the face just inviting Jack to light the fire, at which suggestion Jack also blushes. ('What's going on, sir?') After some talk of rubbing sticks together, Ralph manages to ask if anyone has any matches – for some reason with the bashful air of a penitent in the confessional – and then, a bit later, shouts the same enquiry at Piggy, who has just blundered into the meeting carrying the conch. Only Piggy doesn't appear to have read the sinister script, and pleasantly compliments the rest of the boys on building such a big fire ('My! You've made a big heap, haven't you?').

These sorts of exchanges don't exactly have pupils on the edge of their seats. It's also probably harder for school children today to relate to the descent into savagery, given the current educational climate: on the one hand they are surrounded by positive messages like the ubiquitous 'Aim High, Work Hard, Be Kind' – girls' schools tend to be especially big on 'kindness' – whilst, in their English lessons, their teacher expects them to be interested in a journey towards the child's heart of darkness. It was easier in the seventies and eighties to believe in the boys' savage behaviour when you could play British Bulldog at break and lunchtime in the school playground. In the fortnight leading up to the 1977 FA Cup Final between Liverpool and Manchester United, the normal game of lunchtime football was replaced by a period of intensely tribal hand-to-hand combat between the two sets of supporters. This wasn't in Toxteth or Moss Side, but at a primary school in leafy Canterbury, and might help to account for the novel's place in the school curriculum. Like a school assembly, its message is loud and clear: if you don't follow the rules this is how you'll end up.

But whether such dire warnings are still relevant today is rather less clear. In my daughter's last year at primary school a few years ago, the head teacher banned all ball and running games in the playground. She also introduced 'friendship benches' towards which lonely souls could gravitate in search of company from specially chosen 'friendship monitors'. Only Piggy, of the boys on the island, is obviously friendship monitor material. At the start of the novel he stays behind with the younger boys when Ralph, Jack and Simon go off exploring the island. He tries to tag along after the others but is told, in no uncertain terms, that he's not explorer material, that four's a crowd, and to go back and collect names. At the posh girls' school, the back row emitted a chorus of 'Ah bless' every time Piggy said anything on the old black and white film. You can imagine Piggy in a modern secondary school knuckling down to the injunction 'Aim High, Work Hard, Be Kind'; but by the end of the novel the majority of the boys have gone over to the dark side and a rather different three-part slogan: 'Kill the beast! Cut his throat! Spill his blood!'

On Teaching Practice in 1992 I hadn't yet had the benefit of my old Head of Department's advice. Instead of trying to deliver the story I concentrated on trying to look clever, with fairly disastrous results. When the course tutor, Colin, came to observe me teaching the novel to Year 10, I threw the kitchen sink into my lesson plan and achieved total confusion. From the front of the classroom I could hear Colin talking to the girls on the back row about what they had been asked to do, and then each one admitting they hadn't the slightest idea.

This wasn't a lesson I could dust off and use again after making minor tweaks and improvements. The ideas, along with the industrial quantity of photocopying, went in the bin on the advice of Colin, who, at the end of the lesson, sat me down and articulated some of the questions the class had shared with him. What, for example, had *Bunty*, an old-fashioned girls' comic and the obscure intertextual link around which I had built the lesson, got to do with *Lord of the Flies*? I don't know the answer to this question now, and possibly didn't then, but I can recall the lesson being an unmitigated disaster.

Coral Island might have been a better choice of sister text than *Bunty*, given the obvious links. Ralph and Jack take their names from fearless adventurers Ralph Rover and Jack Martin, though it isn't clear how Piggy is related to their friend Peterkin Gay. Like *Bunty*, but unlike *Lord of the Flies*, *Coral Island* also has a female character – the fair Avatea, who, of course, needs saving by the intrepid English boys. The original Jack is a comparatively honourable figure, and is more concerned with preventing the tribal chief from 'making a long pig' of Avatea than spearing helpless piglets: 'Besides having become champions for this girl once before it behoves us as true knights, not to rest until we set her free; at least all the heroes in all the story books I have ever read would count it a foul disgrace to leave such a work unfinished.'

But in the flesh this Jack is more of a rough diamond than chivalrous knight (or privately educated head chorister) and doesn't waste any gallantry on the native female lead.

'Ah here you are,' said Jack as Avatea approached.

'I understand leetl English,' said Avatea in a low voice.

'Why, where did you pick up English?' exclaimed Jack, amazed; 'you were dumb as a stone when I saw you last.'

By the time that I next locked horns with *Lord of the Flies* I had learned some of the survival strategies used by teachers to get through an hour of coexistence with a class of unruly teenagers. The penny had finally dropped that if they could understand the work you were setting, there was a much better chance of them doing it, rather than simply mucking about. It also helped that I wasn't trying to read the novel this time – but just selected a few extracts, alongside the film, to give the Year 8 Island Project at least a veneer of literary challenge. Without it the Island Project consisted of a succession of pointless tasks from a cheap-looking textbook: draw an island and label it, design and label a shelter, write a diary entry for day one on the island etc., etc. On reflection my big idea wasn't really any more sophisticated – fusing the boys' descent into savagery with the then popular ITV show *Gladiators*. I asked the boys in my class (it was a boys' school) to devise their own bloodthirsty gladiatorial challenges and contests. This could also be padded out with diagrams and labels, and, for those who finished first, was the subject of live, sports-style commentary, recorded on an old-fashioned tape recorder in the stock cupboard. Inevitably, without the civilising influence of adult supervision, some of the live combat turned nasty. Serious injuries were inflicted and lives were lost, requiring – the English teacher in me decided – a follow-up lesson on obituary writing, and, a few lessons later, a full funeral service with boys giving their tearful orations from a lectern borrowed from the school hall, and to the mournful accompaniment of another boy playing the organ.

Usually, a black and white film is greeted by moans and groans, and most of the class switching off. With this group, however, the old film of *Lord of the Flies* had one important advantage – Malleson, a particularly squeamish boy, who fainted at the sight of blood, could watch it without passing out and slipping silently under his desk, as he had done during *Of Mice and*

Men when Lennie crushes Curley's hand. ('Sir, Mally's gone again. Shall I fetch Mrs Thompson?')

Rather more sophisticated lesson plans were required at the posh girls' school. Not only were they paying to hear me talk about a book I didn't like, but they were two years older and it was one of their exam texts. I was relieved to find that they had already covered the first three chapters. I had wondered how a fifteen-year-old girl, conscious of their weight, might react to the relentlessly insensitive treatment of Piggy in Chapter One. The first description of Piggy ('the fat boy') concludes by telling us that he is 'very fat'. There are then another eight references to him being fat on pages two and three, and when Piggy undresses and takes to the water he is described, uncharitably, as 'palely and fatly naked'.

As mentioned previously, there is a neat thematic divide in the novel and plenty of heavy and less than subtle symbolism for students to trawl through. The challenge is to not reduce everything to these two opposing sides – civilisation and democracy versus barbarism and dictatorship – and the instruction 'Divide your page into two and find quotes/make notes for each column...'

The novel gives teachers plenty of scope to display their mastery of the subtext. The description of the choir in Chapter One is a case in point and provoked the first 'Sir, are you sure you're not reading too much into this?' when I suggested their uniform wouldn't have looked out of place at the Nuremberg rallies. Admittedly, they aren't goose stepping, but they do march along the beach in step, still wearing their sinister black cloaks, which are emblazoned with a silver cross on the left breast, exactly where it was positioned on the uniform of an SS officer. And there was, understandably, a similar reaction when I invoked Boris Johnson and the Health Secretary Matt Hancock, at the daily five o'clock COVID press conference, in order to underline the political dimension of Ralph's messaging at the meeting in Chapter Five, as he tries to find words sufficiently simple so that even the 'littluns would understand what the assembly was about'.

Despite the gravity of the boys' situation, I found it hard to get this class of Year 10 girls to take it very seriously. Lines like 'Yours is a big one' didn't help, and nor did asking them to read this sort of exchange out loud:

'Sit down!'
'Shut up!'
'Take the conch!'
'Sod you!'
'Shut up!'

And then Simon, of all people, at the same meeting, comes out with a random question about the rudest thing that any of them know. Any class still awake will want to know the 'one crude expressive syllable' that Jack gives as his answer. The clue is in the equally unhelpful next line: 'Release was like an orgasm... The hunters were screaming with delight.'

Chapter Two

An Inspector Calls

An Inspector Calls is a much easier read than *Lord of the Flies* and is currently probably the most popular choice of Modern Text for GCSE English Literature. The cast is helpfully small – just the Inspector and the four members of the Birling family, plus Sheila's fiancé Gerald Croft – whom the Inspector then questions and finds to be all in some way responsible for the death of a young woman, Eva Smith, who has 'swallowed a lot of strong disinfectant'. There's now also a good BBC film version, so there's no need to show the 1954 black and white film with Alastair Sim as an extremely ghostly Inspector Goole, perversely and confusingly renamed Inspector Poole.

The play is fairly straightforward and there are just a couple of tricky issues to navigate when reading aloud with a class. Mr Birling's long, blustering speeches prior to the Inspector's arrival require a confident reader (or the teacher), and preferably one who can do a regional accent. This should really be a Midlands accent, possibly Brummie – the stage directions tell us that the play takes place in the Birlings' dining room, at their house in Brumley, a city somewhere in the North Midlands – but is better suited to a cantankerous Yorkshire 'I know what I like – I like what I know' persona. And then another highly competent reader is required to read the part of the Inspector. The behaviour stipulated in the stage directions – '*cutting in massively*' and '*massively taking charge*' – doesn't come naturally to most fifteen-year-olds, and so the part tends to go to a high-flyer (if available) or the teacher. And someone has to get the part of Edna, the maid. Edna appears briefly in Act One to announce the arrival of the Inspector, and then gets just one more line near the end to announce Gerald's return ('It's Mr Croft'). Those who've volunteered to read a part often flick ahead to see how much their character says. Not much if you're Edna.

With one particularly difficult class of Year 10 boys there was a much longer list of obstacles to getting through the reading – specifically their reluctance/inability to find a given page in the text, or in some cases, even open the book. For one particularly disastrous lesson, I provided a list on the whiteboard of the pages we were working through chronologically, plus the first line of the selected speech, and a description of where they could find it on the page – top, bottom, middle etc. This wasn't enough and progress was painfully slow, and made slower by a succession of interruptions: the community policeman attached to the school withdrawing one of the boys and then releasing him back into the room a couple of minutes later; two boys in the front row constantly asking what page we were on; another boy in the front row combing his hair with what looked like a very small garden fork; boys needing to borrow a pen or leave the room for tissues or to go to the toilet.

It is tempting after a dismal lesson with one group to open up to another more mature and sympathetic class, and vent fury and frustration, but it was probably a mistake to share my incredulity at the difficulty this Year 10 class had finding the right page in *An Inspector Calls* with the top set in Year 11. After that, whenever we were jumping between bits of their exam text, as soon as I told them which page to turn to, one of the class would very politely ask, 'What page, sir?' And if I didn't immediately twig that this was a wind-up, there would be a short pause and then someone else would pipe up, 'Sorry sir, what page was that?', and then perhaps someone else, until the penny dropped to loud cheers.

It is easy to make a slightly corny comparison between the 'chain' of responsibility in *An Inspector Calls* and the behaviour of your pupils – how it might affect other students in the class etc. I resorted to this after the hopeless reading lesson with the difficult class of Year 10 boys. Having drawn a chain on the board and – I thought – hammered home the point with some force, their next lesson began reasonably quietly. However, things soon began to unravel. A brief passage of sensible discussion was interrupted by the late arrival of one of the most difficult characters in the group, who shuffled in only semi-conscious, apparently unable to speak. The zombie look was enhanced by heavy bandages on his writing hand, which he set about unwrapping as soon as he sat down.

This lesson was supposed to be on Gerald Croft, the rather bland fiancé of Sheila Birling, but was enlivened by a number of unrelated subplots. Just as I completed the introduction, another boy came in late, brushed past me and furiously squared up to another member of the class, whom he accused of writing something about him, or I suspect his girlfriend, on the wall of the boys' toilets. I hurried him out to the Duty Manager and left him to investigate the incendiary toilet text. Back in the classroom, another boy announced that he was going home at lunchtime because he was feeling unwell. I encouraged him to go to the Welfare Room where his not working wouldn't disturb the rest of the class, but he was determined to stay and huddled down into the folds of his coat. Someone else produced a small metal tin of something they claimed was medicinal for the boy's headache. The bandaged latecomer then set about trying to open it whilst simultaneously complaining about his injured hand/wrist, which was preventing him from doing any work. When he finally got the lid off, the tin seemed to contain pungent axle grease, which he set about applying to the temples of his ailing friend.

Conscious that previous attempts to get this class to take notes had ended in failure, in one lesson I provided everything on a sheet, which they just had to cut out and arrange in their books. The young Teaching Assistant supporting me gave me a look which seemed to say, 'I can't see the point of this'/'This is too babyish', but ended up having to stick one boy's quotes down for him. The subject of the lesson was gender inequality and representation in the play. I introduced the topic by showing them a short film about the death of the suffragette Emily Davison, who ran in front of the King's horse at the Derby in 1913. If I thought this would have a sobering effect or give some of them pause for thought, I was wrong. Freed from the need to think or write, some of the boys kept up a constant stream of eye-wateringly inappropriate conversation about girls in their social circle. After forty-five minutes one boy had managed to stick one quote into his book. Sensing the teacher's red mist descending, I bundled him out of the class and into the Duty Manager's room before I lost it.

Unfortunately, their rather literal reading of the play meant that the class's prevailing chauvinism went unchallenged. Eric's jarringly casual attitude towards Eva Smith passed without comment: 'I wasn't in love with her or anything – but I liked her – she was pretty and a good sport...' Their way of expressing it had been different but the sentiment was roughly what they'd been saying amongst themselves whilst they pretended to stick down their quotes. There were also nods of agreement with Mr Birling's unreconstructed attitudes on women and clothes in Act One – specifically that they mean much more to women than to men, who, of course, have other ways to achieve self-respect. 'Standard,' one of them said sagely.

Despite their slow and often rancorous reading of the text, this class did warm to the play. They particularly liked the new film, which I watched with them on tenterhooks, waiting for the next outbreak of 'parring' (the exchange of insults). Whilst showing no capacity for creative reading – for making links and seeing connections – in matters of cussing each other they were exceptionally associative in their thinking. There was nothing that couldn't be used to insult their classmates; a couple of silhouetted outlines of the Inspector in the opening frames suggested the extremely prominent nose of one of the class and immediately threatened to cause trouble, and forced me to sit next to the most accomplished cusser in order to keep the peace.

Unfortunately, thanks to Michael Gove's intervention

during his time as Education Secretary, all students now have to sit an exam on their Modern Text as part of GCSE English Literature. However much the teacher sweetens the pill and puts off the inevitable, eventually this means writing a short essay – a very short essay in the case of some of the boys in this class.

To be fair to J B Priestley he makes the play's themes very accessible. The key messages don't exactly require much detective work from the students, delivered as they are in stereo, first by the Inspector, and then again, underlined in red pen, by his faithful assistant, Sheila: 'But these girls aren't cheap labour – they're *people*.' The Inspector even begins his final speech with an exam tip – 'But just remember this' – before the bit about 'millions of Eva Smiths and John Smiths', which nearly gives the game away: Eva's not real, she's a metaphor, like the 'fire and blood and anguish' – the obvious quote to learn at the end of the speech.

The play also allows the teacher to play inspector and tease information out of their class in case they have missed the Inspector's ghoulish credentials or the obvious dramatic irony (the glaring errors in Mr Birling's version of the future) or missed the significance of the key dates (spring, 1912, when the play is set, and October 1946, when the play was first performed in London).

Historical context isn't usually students' strong suit. Most will know (roughly) the years of the two World

Wars, but this class of Year 10 boys wasn't most boys. One member of the class interrupted the film to ask if the play was set in England, which seemed a ridiculous question even by their standards, given the discussion we'd already had. Previously, it was reported back to me by one of their other teachers, two boys in this group had spent an entire lesson arguing over whether you could take a ferry to Mount Everest, so, perhaps, it wasn't such a ridiculous question. Clement Attlee's post-war Labour government, the creation of the NHS and Welfare State, wasn't, therefore, something I could rely on them knowing anything about – cue timeline to copy from the board.

When I studied the play at school in the early 1980s, with the Thatcher government starting to dismantle the state and Mrs Thatcher denying the existence of society, the political message made a lot of sense. Our teacher, a proudly militant northerner, who could easily be led off-topic if we asked questions about coal mining, seemed like an indignant extension of J B Priestley. Teenagers studying the play today will have a tougher job working out the political battle lines after the coronavirus. Just when it seemed that the general election of 1983 – Thatcher versus Michael Foot/ socialism – had been replayed with Johnson and Corbyn in the 2019 election, the victorious Conservatives have been forced by a worldwide pandemic to start behaving like one of Mr Birling's 'cranks' who 'think everybody has to look after everybody else...community and all that nonsense', and outspend and outborrow Labour's much maligned manifesto pledges. Corbyn's magic money tree now belongs to Rishi Sunak, the Conservative Chancellor of the Exchequer.

Chapter Three

Of Mice and Men

'The best laid plans o' mice and men gang-aft-a-gley'

The last bit of this quotation from Robert Burns' poem 'To a Mouse' (full title 'To a Mouse, on Turning Her Up in Her Nest with the Plough') basically means that whatever we do, and however carefully we plan (our lessons), everything will invariably go pear-shaped in the end. There couldn't be a more appropriate text for the life of a school teacher.

My first week as a secondary school teacher, in September 1994, unfortunately coincided with my new school's first Ofsted inspection for five years. I was an NQT, a 'newly qualified teacher'. They wouldn't be interested in what I was doing and probably wouldn't even observe me, my Head of Department told me. In fact, the English inspector visited me on four occasions.

The last of these visits was on Thursday afternoon, by which time the inspection was supposed to have been done and dusted. For that reason, I had judged it safe to put on the film of *Of Mice and Men* for the little bottom Year 11 group I was teaching in period five.

Not only did I not have any learning objectives, or a lesson plan of any sort, because of the wooden floors and high ceilings in my classroom it was virtually impossible to hear what George and Lennie were saying. Ten minutes into the film the inspector walked in and sat down at the back of the room.

Trying not to appear too rattled I let the film play for another couple of minutes and then, very deliberately, stopped it and asked the boys, who had been huddled round the TV, to return to their desks and open their exercise books.

Recalling something my old English teacher had told us about the Garden of Eden/creation symbolism at the start of the novel, I asked the class to draw a lizard, followed by a rabbit.

Had the inspector not left at this point, the rabbit would have been followed by a raccoon, a dog, a deer, and then a man – recreating, I was prepared to argue rather pointlessly, the creation story in the Book of Genesis. As it was, I decided it was safe to put the film back on and let it play for the rest of the lesson.

Despite my contribution to the inspection, I had joined – it was announced on Friday morning – a 'Good' school.

The post-inspection party in the pub next door to the school didn't seem like the right time to ask my

Head of Department what was really on my mind. 'But what am I to teach them?' asks Paul Pennyfeather, the timid hero of Evelyn Waugh's novel *Decline and Fall*.

Despite, or perhaps because of, having completed a PGCE (Post Graduate Certificate of Education), I had no idea what to do with *Of Mice and Men*. The answer from Paul's colleague Captain Grimes – 'Oh, I shouldn't try to teach them anything, not just yet anyway' – wasn't all that far from what my Head of Department did advise when we spoke the following week: 'If I were you I'd read it with them. And they'll like the film.'

This was still my cunning plan over twenty years later when I was visited one morning by the lady on SLT (Senior Leadership Team) responsible for Teaching and Learning. I had completely forgotten that it was our turn for Departmental Evaluation Week and that she was doing a Learning Walk (basically a mini inspection) down the English corridor. I had banked on spending the lesson reading *Of Mice and Men* with possibly a bit of the film thrown in at the end. I was happy for her to think that she would miss the interesting bit of the lesson where the students actually learned something – which I wanted to give the impression I was building up to. This was a Learning Walk, so she couldn't stay for ever, I reasoned, and carried on reading. But rather than move on to another lesson she stayed, and remained for so long that she eventually forced me to show my hand and admit it was going to be one of those reading the book/watching the film lessons.

Of Mice and Men remains an essential rite of passage for any secondary school pupil, although, as it's no longer a GCSE exam text, students are more likely to encounter it in Year 9. Presumably, this makes it more likely that other pupils will innocently repeat my own schoolboy error, reading whorehouse as 'war house', much to the delight of everyone else in the class. It remains the one novel that nearly always manages to engage and/or pacify even the most difficult classes, and English teachers have always resisted any change to the syllabus which doesn't include it as one of the set texts. It consists mainly of dialogue (pupils become restless during long passages of description) and there's the chance to do American accents and a funny voice/your John Malkovich impression for Lennie. There's also a memorable fight scene in which the obnoxious son of the boss (Curley) has his hand crushed by Lennie, which groups of boys will invariably ask you to rewind so that they can watch Curley suffer twice. And as much as pupils enjoy taking the mickey out of each other, they tend to be much more sensitive and generous to those they regard as hard done by or underdogs, and are touched by the plight of the weak characters – Lennie, old Candy, Candy's dog, Crooks, and eventually Curley's wife.

Unfortunately, like a lot of GCSE set texts, the

novel is not a great advert for gender equality, and the problem with some boys taking everything too literally is that they emerge from the novel even more chauvinistic than when they started. As George says prophetically in Chapter Three, just before the ranch hands move on to discussing the local brothels, the Tyler Ranch, with its population of red blooded here today, gone tomorrow farm workers, isn't an ideal situation for a young woman. Curley's wife is the only female on the ranch and, even though she is married to the boss's son, is somewhere near the bottom of the food chain and doesn't even qualify for her own name. Nor does her behaviour exactly break the mould for fifteen-year-old boys, whose role models are Channel 4's *The Inbetweeners*. Having had the temerity to introduce herself to George and Lennie, shortly after their arrival in Chapter Two, George, who is one of the good guys, immediately assumes her intentions must be sexual, and spits out a succession of derogatory metaphors on the theme of loose women as a warning to Lennie to keep his distance. And in Chapter Five, when she gets to unburden herself to Lennie of all people, and we hear a bit more about her, none of it is very helpful for gender politics and representation: she wants to be a film star, she dreams of having nicer clothes, and she likes playing with her hair.

Lennie's (dead) Aunt Clara appears briefly in the final chapter in the form of a hallucination. She is followed shortly after by a giant rabbit, but what should be a very pleasant daydream for rabbit enthusiast Lennie turns sour when the rabbit scolds him in his own voice. The only other female characters mentioned are Susy and a different Clara, the competing brothel owners. There is also a poignant walk-on part for the shepherd bitch in Chapter Five, which seems to feel the death of Curley's wife more keenly than any of the human characters: as soon as she catches the scent of Curley's dead wife the hairs on her back stand up, she lets out a whimper, and goes scuttling back to her puppies. Curley's only thought at the death scene is for Lennie – it's a chance to get even with the great big son-of-a-bitch who busted his hand – and, brushing off his loss, he rushes off to get his gun. And even old Candy can't manage a kind word for the corpse, but sends her off with some more Whore of Babylon-type slurs on her sexual purity.

The rather unsentimental attitude the workers have towards sexual relationships also throws up some interesting and potentially awkward questions in the classroom. In Chapter Three we learn that sexual relations will cost you around two and a half at Old Susy's, ('How much is that, sir?') but that at Clara's place there are men walking out bow-legged because Clara, it seems, is prioritising the interior décor (there's a rug on the floor, a lamp and a phonograph) and isn't looking after the brothel's bread and butter, with physical consequences which take a bit of explaining to a group of school children. Similarly, Curley's glove full of vaseline or why he has taken to eating raw eggs and writing off for patent medicines.

A more serious and sensitive issue is what the teacher does about the fifteen uses of the n-word in reference to Crooks, the stable buck. Last week the BBC apologised for having used it in a news report, even though the BBC claimed it was at the request of the family of a black man, who had suffered racial abuse. The problem was the word (obviously taken from someone else's words) being said by white reporters or presenters. I have never previously edited out the n-word whilst reading *Of Mice and Men* aloud to a class, but this policy now feels out of step, like another case of white privilege. It is obviously something the teacher should discuss with their class first. Or perhaps not, on reflection; apologising for the word and then carrying on and using it fifteen times for reasons of artistic/literary authenticity doesn't seem at all obvious any more.

My old O level class read the book with Mr Jones at some point in the fourth year (Year 10 in new money) but very little of it stayed with me from that first reading. There was no Hollywood film version then, just the musty school editions of the text – hardback covers from Heinemann – which had seen better days. Some of us were called on to read aloud but nobody could do an American accent and Mr Jones read everything in his Yorkshire accent, which is perhaps why the characters never really sprang to life. Lots of their names also seemed fairly similar – Candy, Curley, Crooks, Carlson – and I had no memory of Crooks, the stable buck. Perhaps, like the film version, we also edited out parts of the text we didn't want to read, like the heartbreaking Chapter Four, which takes place in Crooks' room – basically a small shed that has been built on to the side of the barn. It's Saturday night and we learn from Lennie that everybody else has gone into town – code for the local brothels. Without George around to supervise him, Lennie blunders into Crooks' room with his catchphrase about having seen his light, oblivious to the racial divide and Crooks' territorial rights. Despite not thinking much of his company or intellect, Crooks, rather tragically, also ends up unburdening himself to Lennie. Having shared a poignant story of racial segregation from his childhood, Lennie's considered response is to ask how long it will be before Slim's pups will be old enough for him to pet! Not surprisingly, Crooks takes the opportunity to turn the tables and bully someone else and torments Lennie with the thought that George might not return, but has to backtrack when Lennie loses his temper, mindful of what happened to Curley's hand in Chapter Three.

The gathering of the weak and dispossessed expands with the arrival of old Candy and Curley's wife. The chapter ends with the chilling exchange between Crooks and Curley's wife, which is so unpleasant and hard to read that the film cuts it out altogether. Crooks summons up a brief moment of defiance, and questions her right to wander into his room uninvited, but is stopped in his tracks as Curley's wife drives home the hopelessness of his situation and reminds him of what she can do if he talks. Crooks' defeat is total: having stood up and faced her squarely he now shrinks back down on his bunk and dons his version of an invisibility cloak, hunkering down and hoping that the danger will pass.

Chapter Four features four very different characters/ voices, which is helpful when it comes to class reading. This isn't the case in the bunk house in Chapter Three, where it becomes a challenge for the teacher or volunteers reading to distinguish between the different ranch hands. Lennie is the exception, and also Curley when he explodes into the bunk house towards the end of the chapter. But finding subtly different versions of an American ranch hand for George, Slim, Candy, Whit and Carlson isn't easy and after a while it all seems to merge into one uniform and slightly soporific cowboy drawl.

Having now become something of an itinerant worker myself – five schools in two years – I have started to identify rather gloomily with some of George's lines about life on the road, the stuff about loneliness and not belonging to any place. Candy's survival strategy for life on the ranch – making sure you don't listen and never asking questions – might also apply to the supply teacher at staff meetings and morning briefings, hoping for a quiet life below the radar of SLT whilst they get the money together to pay the mortgage on their own little house.

Despite the novel's bleak pessimism, pupils genuinely enjoy the book. Michael Gove, who oversaw big changes to GCSE specifications during his time as the Conservative Education Secretary, is apparently rather less keen. The *Independent* reported in 2014 that he 'really dislikes' it, before adding that it had been 'studied by 90% of the teenagers taking English Literature in the past'. According to *The Sunday Times* Gove thinks that 'students ought to focus on works by British writers such as Jane Austen and Shakespeare'. It also quoted a Senior Lecturer at King's College London, who described the new specification as 'a syllabus out of the 1940s... rumour has it Mr Gove, who read Literature, designed it himself.'

When Gove gave *Of Mice and Men* the chop for the latest GCSE English Literature specification, it had only been back on the list for a few years, having been dropped at some point around the start of the new millennium. It was a dark day for English teachers and their students when our exam board replaced it for a period with Hemingway's *The Old Man and the Sea*, which has no advantages for the teacher, and virtually none for the reader. Not surprisingly for a novel which largely depicts a man fishing, there also isn't a good film version available. The one I did find was so bad that students opted to read the book instead. Unfortunately, most of the text is so turgid that it can only be digested in short bursts. One class attempted to lighten the mood by exploiting its Hispanic setting, and read the whole thing in the voice of Manuel from *Fawlty Towers*. The only related activity which vaguely engaged the class was a mass arm-wrestle – a recreation of the old man's marathon with the 'Negro from Cienfuegos'.

Both texts pit the spiritual dimension against the physical or material. The inevitability of physical defeat/our mortality is the cheery conclusion at the end of both novels, but at least in *Of Mice and Men* there is some attempt to soften the blow with the final moving rendition of George and Lennie's bedtime story about the little house and living off the fat of the land. In *The Old Man and the Sea* there is the companionship between the boy and the old man and an obvious sense of handover ('I can learn and you can teach me everything') but it's fairly obvious the old man's not up to it. The final depressing image is of the 'long back bone of the great fish, that was now just garbage waiting to go out with the sea'. Earlier we are told that 'he sailed the skiff to make his home port as well and intelligently as he could', which a number of teenage readers have questioned, along the lines of, 'But sir, isn't he sailing back with just a head and a skeleton? That's not very intelligent!'

And then, as if eyeing up a Nobel Prize, Hemingway can't resist framing the old man's walk back home, carrying the mast up the hill, as a Christ with the cross moment, and when he sleeps it's 'with his arms out straight and the palms of his hands up'.

Students tend to be much more protective of Lennie, who is also about to meet his end. Even though they have known this is coming – pupils like to scrawl 'Lennie dies in the end' at the top of the first page to spoil it for the next pupil who has that book – it still comes as a bit of a blow, and they appreciate George's/ Steinbeck's efforts to give Lennie a good send-off. In the film version George shoots him – like Candy's dog, right in the back of his head – just as Lennie blurts out the word *rabbits*, but in the book there's nearly another page in which Lennie is wrapped in cotton wool and almost delivered to the front door of the little house, which George tells him to look for across the river, whilst he steadies the gun behind him in his shaking hand.

Chapter Four

Pride and Prejudice

An extremely agreeable way of spending the summer term is with Jane Austen's novel *Pride and Prejudice*. The BBC adaptation takes the strain on hot afternoons (and fills up about six hours of lesson time) and even some of the most difficult students tend to respond enthusiastically.

During one spell of particularly hot weather, the boys in my Year 10 class (not the difficult one) arrived to lessons after lunch so hot and sweaty and fractious from running around in the playground that it was virtually impossible to interest them in any work. And whilst I was attempting to teach them *Pride and Prejudice* – a novel in which the characters' idea of exercise is a 'turn around the room' – the first ten minutes of several lessons was spent remonstrating with boys who had removed their shirts and socks.

There has sometimes been a bit of initial resistance to *Pride and Prejudice*, along the lines of 'this looks old', 'my mum likes it', 'it's a girls' book' – but the first chapter generally dispels these doubts. It is short and funny, and, as in *Of Mice and Men*, the description is minimal – you don't feel the class nodding off as you drone on through a long passage of narrative – and it usually goes down very well. A Year 9 group at a high achieving girls' (state) school proved to be an exception, but this class had also rubbished *Of Mice and Men* in my first lesson with them (whilst enthusing about ITV's *Love Island*), which had immediately set alarm bells ringing.

Another complaint I have heard is that it is too wordy. The famous first sentence of *Pride and Prejudice* might appear so – 'It is a truth universally acknowledged, that a single man in possession of a good fortune, must be in want of a wife.' – and it obviously isn't the sort of language you hear in the playground or in the corridor, but at least you reach the end of the sentence still remembering how it started. The same can't always be said of Austen's famous contemporary Sir Walter Scott. The first two sentences of his novel *Rob Roy*, published the year of Austen's death, are a case in point:

> You have requested me, my dear friend, to bestow some of that leisure with which Providence has blessed the decline of my life, in registering the hazards and difficulties which attended its commencement. The recollection of those adventures, as you are pleased to term

them, has indeed left upon my mind a chequered and varied feeling of pleasure and of pain, mingled, I trust, with no slight gratitude and veneration to the Disposer of human events, who guided my early course through much risqué and labour, that the ease with which he has blessed my prolonged life, might seem softer from remembrance and contrast.

As well as writing historical novels, Scott was an advocate, a judge, and a poet, and juggled his writing with his day job as Sheriff-Depute of Selkirkshire. He was also a prominent Tory and an active member of the Highland Society. None of these are exactly a guarantee against pomposity and verbal diarrhoea. By comparison – and also in comparison with many other later-nineteenth-century novels – Austen's voice sounds positively modern and is full of pithy one-liners and put-downs: 'Lady Lucas was a very good kind of woman', 'Mr Collins was not a sensible man', and 'Lady Catherine was a tall, large woman, with strongly marked features, which might once have been handsome'. Despite this lightness of touch, it isn't possible, as it is with *Of Mice and Men*, to read the entire novel aloud in class, which means relying on students to read some of the novel at home. The last time I naively set summer reading – only up to the end of Volume One/page 128 – just two members of the thirty-two-strong top set obliged. This was at a boys' school, where it wouldn't have been cool to admit to having done any reading during the summer holiday, but stiff questioning in the first couple of lessons back confirmed that most of the class hadn't opened the book since our last lesson in July. On reflection, promising them that they would acquire a full understanding of the semicolon if they read the book probably wasn't the way to sell it to a group of teenage boys. And the semicolon is often responsible for the wordier moments in the novel – like this bit from Chapter Four, describing Elizabeth's negative reaction to the Bingley sisters: 'Elizabeth listened in silence, but was not convinced; their behaviour at the assembly had not been calculated to please in general; and with more quickness of observation and less pliancy of temper than her sister, and with a judgement too unassailed by any attention to herself, she was very little disposed to approve them.'

Words like 'pliancy', 'unassailed' and 'little disposed' belong to a semantic field that is recognisably Jane Austen's, but one which is distinctly unfamiliar to most students, and can inspire groans of pain from boys on the back row – 'This is moist, sir!' This was also the reaction to 'felicity', 'inclination', 'deficiency', 'amiable', 'acquaintance' and 'matrimony'.

'Moist' was also this class's verdict on Mr Collins.

He also had, according to them – at least in the BBC adaptation – a 'dead trim' (dodgy haircut). They were right on both counts but I soon learned not to rely on their judgement. After their first lesson on *Pride and Prejudice* one boy came to see me to tell me he didn't understand it. We'd only read the first chapter, which is two and a half pages long, watched a bit of the first episode and briefly discussed the rather different view of marriage in 1800.

'What don't you understand?' I asked.

'Just don't understand it, sir.'

And later when we got to the end of the novel and the heated exchange between Elizabeth and Lady Catherine, one boy asked, apparently seriously, 'Will Lady Catherine kill Darcy when she finds out about him and Elizabeth?' This was followed by an even more bizarre question: 'Was Elizabeth drunk when she said yes to Mr Darcy?'

This class also managed to make a mockery of my *social ladder* activity. What I had thought to be a reasonably watertight lesson floundered in the face of confusion and apathy. Having been at pains to assure them that there was no wrong answer for this task – positioning the characters in the novel on their rung of the ladder/place in the social hierarchy – I wasn't prepared to find the Bennets' housemaid (Hill) positioned two rungs above Mr Bennet, gentleman landowner and her employer.

As with any self-respecting GCSE set text, there is a neat thematic divide in *Pride and Prejudice* which separates the goodies from the baddies, and again encourages the two-column approach when students make notes on the characters. It is also the title of Austen's first published novel, *Sense and Sensibility*, which features the chalk and cheese Dashwood sisters – Elinor, the sensible and quietly stoical elder sister, and Marianne, the reckless romantic. It is difficult to explain to fans of *Love Island* that words like 'fancy' and 'romance' are bad words in a Jane Austen novel; and even harder to explain that Marianne's reward/ punishment for falling for the dashing Willoughby is marriage to a man more than twice her age, Colonel Brandon. And after some unsuccessful dabbling with fancy and romance, twenty-one-year-old Emma Woodhouse ('handsome, clever and rich'), the heroine of Austen's novel *Emma*, is also married off to a much older man – 'Mr Knightley, a sensible man about seven or eight-and-thirty'.

However warm it might be in the classroom during the summer term, there is nothing in *Pride and Prejudice* to get steamed up about or set the teenage pulse racing. Arch representatives of the Augustan Age, or Age of Reason, like Mr Darcy and Mr Knightley, must appear rather dry sticks to teenage readers, and so it is tempting to inject a bit more heat into the central love story. When Colin Firth (Mr Darcy in the

BBC version) strips to his undergarments and dives into his lake at Pemberley, he is, I've found myself saying to various classes, obviously boiling with lust and trying to cool off. And that's what the fencing lessons were all about in the previous scene – trying to work through his powerful feelings for Elizabeth. But the problem with saying anything in a lesson is that students are likely to remember it and repeat it in their final exam, and ignore the fact that this never happens in the novel. The nearest Mr Darcy comes to anything physical in the text is during his first proposal to Elizabeth: 'His complexion became pale with anger, and the disturbance of his mind was visible in every feature.' But even then, his Captain Sensible side kicks in to prevent any loss of dignity: 'He was struggling for the appearance of composure, and would not open his lips, till he believed himself to have attained it.' Even at the end of the novel, when his second proposal is accepted, all he's allowed is an 'expression of heartfelt delight'. There's no passionate embrace and students have to wait for the final frame of the final episode of the BBC version for a sealing kiss – a slightly awkward coming together beneath the protruding rim of Mr Darcy's top hat, something that is never mentioned in the text.

The more recent film version, starring Keira Knightley, goes much further in sexing up the novel. In Chapter Eight Elizabeth's petticoat creates something of a scandal at Netherfield by being 'six inches deep in mud'; in Joe Wright's film she heads off at dawn into the fields wearing not much more than her petticoat, or nightie, for her date with destiny/Darcy towards the end of the story. There is also an alternative ending for the American audience, which shows a loved-up Darcy and Elizabeth, neither wearing very much, floating around on what looks like a giant shell on a torch-lit lake at Pemberley, which even the *Love Island* fans found ridiculous.

With such a straight-laced text, it isn't surprising that a class of sex-obsessed teenage boys will look for things that aren't really there. One class of boys in the lower sixth (Year 12) studying *Pride and Prejudice* alongside *Emma* for a unit called the Comic Perspective, seemed to think it was their job to provide the comedy, and took great pleasure from every reference in the novels to 'intercourse', of which there are many. For example, this suggestion – as they saw it – of Darcy's colourful past in Chapter Forty-Four: 'people, with whom any intercourse a few months ago would have been a disgrace'. And Aunt Gardiner's steamy night out during their stay in Lambton: 'the evening was spent in the satisfactions of an intercourse renewed after many years'. And when Mr Woodhouse, of all people, is responsible in Chapter Twelve for the 'ejaculation in Emma's ear', they thought it was Christmas come early. This group would also complain that the sound on the film was either too loud or too quiet, and only be happy when the volume setting, which went from one to a hundred, settled on sixty-nine, whereupon there would be a loud cheer.

Mr Collins is the most obvious comedy gold in the novel and his clumsy proposal to Elizabeth in Chapter Nineteen tends to be the extract most closely studied. He is also her cousin, which is generally regarded as being beyond the pale by squeamish GCSE students, and Austen's obligatory materialistic clergyman. Students can't help but feel for Elizabeth the minute she's singled out by Mr Collins for special attention. Having originally selected her sister Jane, first, we are told, in age and beauty, he switches to Elizabeth during 'a quarter of an hour's tête-à-tête with Mrs Bennet'. Dickens would probably have made a great song and dance of Mr Collins' odious pragmatism. Jane Austen does it in a half a line – 'done while Mrs Bennet was stirring the fire'.

Students enjoy seeing him get his comeuppance when Elizabeth turns him down and even difficult classes of Year 10 boys become indignant on her behalf ('This guy's a wasteman!') when Mr Collins turns the screws with 'it is by no means certain that another offer of marriage may ever be made you'. And there is gleeful satisfaction – 'You've been mugged off, mate!' – when Elizabeth walks out.

At some point in the 1990s I attempted, in a foolish

bid for relevance and street credibility, to link Mr Collins' reliance on convention in the proposal scene with Mark Renton's encounter with Diane outside the night club in the film *Trainspotting*. I may have been influenced by the Cool Britannia-flavoured hype surrounding Irvine Welsh's novel *Trainspotting*, which was marketed along the lines of 'this is the best novel ever'. All of my contemporaries had seen the film but I didn't know anyone who had read the book, much of which was written in impenetrable Scottish dialect/slang. Students are always happy to watch a film, especially when it's a certificate 18 (justified on this occasion by it only being a short clip), but they showed rather less interest in *Trainspotting* than Mr Collins, and I should have stuck to my Head of Department's advice – stick to the text and don't try to be too clever.

Chapter Five

A Christmas Carol

Reading books and writing about them (English Literature) has always struggled for credibility by comparison with other more heavyweight academic subjects. It lacks the obviously relevant applications of the Sciences and Mathematics, and doesn't quite have the gravitas of History. Only Geography, often taught to the lower years by PE teachers/the textbook, and RE sit lower than English Literature in most pupils' pecking order. The compensation for English teachers of teaching a relatively lightweight subject was the chance to make lessons enjoyable – to be popular. Without a body of knowledge to deliver or a syllabus to get through, the English teacher could be a more relaxed, humane figure – like Mr Farthing in *Kes*, who can hand the stick of chalk over to a 'bad-un' like Billy Casper and let him do the lesson on his 'awk' (his hawk). My first Head of Department told a lot of (often unrepeatable) stories and showed a lot of films, and was the sort of teacher celebrities single out when interviewed about their school days – 'Mr so and so was great. He let us watch loads of films. But he was a really good teacher…'

English teachers, generally, fared well in the 'my favourite teacher' scenarios, but that was before Michael Gove made it compulsory for all pupils to sit final GCSE exams on a nineteenth-century novel, a Shakespeare play, a twentieth-century literary text, a themed unit of poetry and unseen poetry. As a result, English teachers are now responsible for some of the most boring lessons in a student's school life. Notable amongst these, are those devoted to *A Christmas Carol*, currently the most popular choice of nineteenth-century novel. At the high-achieving girls' state school, the exclusive top set studied *Pride and Prejudice* or *Jane Eyre*. The rest did *A Christmas Carol*, a sort of bargain basement substitute, complete with a Jim Carrey animated film. But since the introduction of the new Govian English Literature GCSE in 2015, in many schools, everyone does it.

The obvious advantage of *A Christmas Carol* is its length, or rather shortness – less than ninety pages in the cheap paperback editions favoured by schools. Beyond that it is difficult to account for its popularity. For Gove and disciples of Gove, it may represent a treasured piece of our cultural heritage – a rite of passage for teenagers through a sentimental theme park of Merry England, akin to taking part in Morris dancing or attending a village fete. There are exceptions, but most of the novel speaks/sings to us in the fake jollity of a bustling street scene from a Broadway musical: 'The Grocers! Oh, the Grocers!' or 'Hallo! A great deal of steam!'

It begins promisingly: 'Marley was dead, to begin with... Old Marley was as dead as a doornail.' But just as you've settled the class and got their attention with this sombre announcement, Dickens changes paragraph and switches into what appears to be an attempt at comedy, for which the signal is often the exclamation mark ('Mind!'), and ponders why one would be 'dead as a doornail', not as a 'coffin-nail' – 'the deadliest piece of ironmongery in the trade'. Quite understandably, any interest the class might have felt, begins to drain away at this point.

In Stave Three the exclamation mark ('Think of that!') is the signal for another attempt at comedy, on the theme of Scrooge's clerk, Bob Cratchit: 'Bob had but fifteen "Bob" a week himself; he pocketed on Saturdays but fifteen copies of his Christian name...'

This isn't helpful in terms of students' reckoning of the past. Many are inclined to dismiss anything that looks old, and this extract is likely to confirm their belief that comedy began with *Friends* in the 1990s – just after *The Muppet Christmas Carol* (1992), which also attempted a comic treatment of the Cratchit family, casting Kermit the Frog as Bob Cratchit and Miss Piggy as his wife Emily (plain Mrs Cratchit in the text).

My recollection, from the start of my teaching career in the 1990s, is that *A Christmas Carol* was something English teachers used in the last couple of weeks of the autumn term before finishing for the Christmas holiday – just a few extracts and then the Muppet film for the last week of term. It didn't occur to any of my colleagues to read all of it or take it very seriously, let alone spend a whole term studying it for the final exam.

It may lack comedy value, drama and interesting characters, but *A Christmas Carol* does have the kind of clear moral message you get from a school assembly – like a nativity play for teenagers, now that they're too big for dressing up in towels and dressing gowns for the part of the shepherds. But given his evident concern for the plight of the poor, Dickens sometimes has a funny way of showing it, and can come across as a bit of a cold fish. The flowery style he employs generally in his fiction, and here in his article 'A Nightly Scene in London', may be perfect for an eight-mark language analysis question but doesn't exactly convey solidarity with his subjects – five homeless people waiting to be admitted to the workhouse: 'Five great beehives, covered with rags – five dead bodies taken out of graves, tied neck and heels, and covered with rags – would have looked like those five bundles upon which the rain rained down in the public street.' The same rather showy hyperbole ('This is long, sir!') is also used to describe 'Ignorance' and 'Want', the boy and girl at the end of Stave Three: 'Yellow, meagre, ragged, scowling, wolfish... Where angels might have sat enthroned, devils lurked, and glared out menacing. No change, no degradation, no perversion of humanity in any grade, through all the mysteries of wonderful creation, has monsters half so horrible and dread.'

In order to make links to context in their answers (Assessment Objective 3) many students will have been told that Dickens' father spent three months inside Marshalsea debtors' prison, and that during this period the twelve-year-old Dickens was employed in a blacking warehouse, labelling bottles. This information may surprise readers in light of the consistently patronising tone Dickens uses in reference to the poor in *A Christmas Carol*. In Stave Three the Londoners clearing snow from their roof-tops do so under a 'gloomy' sky and in streets 'choked up with a dingy mist...whose heavier particles descended in a shower of sooty atoms' – but they couldn't be happier. There was 'an air of cheerfulness abroad' and 'the people who were shovelling away on the house-tops were jovial and full of glee'.

The Cratchit family also emerge from the breathless account of their Christmas Dinner as rather diminished characters. More exclamation marks herald the arrival of the Christmas pudding:

Suppose it should not be done enough! Suppose it should break in turning out! Suppose somebody should have got over the wall of the backyard and stolen it, while they were merry with the goose... All sorts of horrors were supposed.

Hallo! A great deal of steam! The pudding was out of the copper.

A smell like a washing-day... That was the pudding!

The honourable exception, and a rare passage of restraint, follows Tiny Tim's imagined death in Stave Four. For once, Dickens lets the events speak for themselves: 'The mother laid her work upon the table, and put her hand up to her face.' Bob Cratchit's grief for his 'little child' is also affecting – 'He broke down all at once' – if rather short-lived. Plucky poor person that he is, he makes a full recovery eight lines later: 'He was reconciled to what had happened, and went down again quite happy.' Ditto the miners 'who labour in the bowels of the earth'; despite the 'howling of the wind upon the barren waste' they are not permitted to feel sorry for themselves but put their best clothes on, form a 'cheerful company' around a 'glowing fire' and sing Christmas songs. And the lighthouse keepers, who join 'horny hands over the rough table at which they were sat' ('Are they batty men, sir?'), wish each other Merry Christmas, and also start singing.

Unfortunately, this doesn't tend to trigger the sympathy pupils usually feel for characters they regard as hard done by or underdogs, because, unlike Joe Gargery and Magwitch in *Great Expectations*, they aren't really characters, and certainly not the rounded characters for which nineteenth-century novels are celebrated.

At around 450 pages long, *Great Expectations* is, quite understandably, viewed as a bridge too far for many students. It may be too long for an exam text but there is now an excellent three-part BBC film, which holds the interest of the most challenging classes – even the difficult class of Year 10 boys. There were numerous points of confusion during the screening. Many of these related to the shadowy figure of Old Orlick, who they referred to as 'Zombieman' – a character, they informed me, from one of their favourite computer games – and I found myself having to adopt this for the sake of clarity. Estella elicited mixed reactions. 'She's peng' (attractive) was the general view of the young Estella, but there was disagreement about the mature character – or rather the actress playing her in the film. And for all their bravado, most of the boys in the group seemed to be unnerved by Miss Havisham's dry skin and manic hand rubbing.

Halfway through the second episode of *Great Expectations* a boy in this class interrupted the film to denounce another boy on the back row as an 'obese panda'. I stopped the film and asked him to go to the Duty Manager, which he did very slowly and via an altercation with a boy in the front row, which required him to be physically restrained and escorted the rest of the way. When I explained to the Duty Manager, after the lesson, that he'd called another boy 'obese' he flatly denied it. 'No, I didn't, I swear!'

This went back and forth for a bit until I repeated the charge a fifth time ('I distinctly heard you call him obese') – and the boy shouted back in exasperation, 'I did not call him a beast.'

The Duty Manager looked at me pityingly from beneath raised eyebrows, awaiting my next move, which was to spell out o-b-e-s-e. 'Did you call him an obese panda?'

'Yes, sir.'

But the storm had passed – our combined indignation disarmed by farce and confusion.

The class managed to watch the final moments of the film in respectful near silence. The new film delivers a straightforwardly happy ending by engineering a swift reunion between Pip and Estella, whereas the novel makes them wait eleven years. To pad out the final lesson I read the last chapter to them and attempted to introduce the concept of pathetic fallacy via some of the rather obvious imagery – Pip's 'mist' clearing with the help of Estella's 'moonlight'. One boy bemoaned the wordiness of these three pages, comparing them unfavourably to *The Diary of a Wimpy Kid*, his preferred reading, and I couldn't really argue with him.

Tedious though they are, Dickens' grotesque caricatures of ignorance and want in *A Christmas Carol* at least feel like his department. Even harder to stomach is the infantile final chapter – Stave Five, The End of It – where Scrooge suddenly becomes deliriously happy.

At the end of Evelyn Waugh's novel, *A Handful of Dust*, Tony Last is held prisoner somewhere in the South American jungle by the sinister Mr Todd and made to read Dickens to him in the afternoons. 'We will not have any Dickens today...' says Mr Todd when Tony wakes at the very end of the novel with a thumping headache, 'but tomorrow, and the day after that, and the day after that.' The final nail in Tony's coffin is Mr Todd's suggestion that they read *Little Dorrit* again: 'There are passages in that book I can never hear without the temptation to weep.' I can't be the only English teacher who feels like this when required to read the following lines to a group of bemused teenagers: 'The chuckle with which he said this, and the chuckle with which he paid for the turkey, and the chuckle with which he paid for the cab, and the chuckle with which he recompensed the boy, were only to be exceeded by the chuckle with which he sat down breathless in his chair again, and chuckled till he cried.'

And perhaps Michael Gove, who generally sounds like a voice-over from a GCSE moderation video, could model the class reading for the church bell in Stave Five – 'Clash, clash, hammer; ding, dong, bell! Bell, dong, ding; hammer, clang, clash! Oh, glorious, glorious!' – and then explain what this turkey is doing on the syllabus. 'Bah! Humbug!'

Chapter Six

The Adventure
of the Speckled Band

Another Victorian writer promoted to the set text list in Michael Gove's reshuffle is the creator of Sherlock Holmes, Arthur Conan Doyle. This has coincided with the hit TV series *Sherlock*, starring Benedict Cumberbatch, which means that school pupils are usually prepared to give the stories a go, even if they are old and a bit longwinded. They also seem to like not having to wade through an obvious thematic scheme – the sort of clear moral message they get in *A Christmas Carol* or *An Inspector Calls*, or in their school assemblies. Instead, Holmes is introduced as an on-off cocaine user at the start of 'A Scandal in Bohemia', the first story in *The Adventures of Sherlock Holmes* – 'a waste man!' in the opinion of one admiring Year 10 class.

The formulaic aspect of the stories is better suited to recreative writing than exam study or literary analysis, and the most I have ever attempted is reading the whole of 'The Adventure of the Speckled Band', followed by pupils writing their own story. An authentic recreation means narrating their story in the voice of Holmes' 'intimate friend and associate, Dr Watson' and starting with Watson thumbing back through the pages of his case notes. Then the scene needs to be set, at 221b Baker Street. This might involve mentioning Mrs Hudson (Holmes' landlady, who hardly ever appears) or the option of some stiff masculine banter between Holmes and Watson as they wait for their next case. At the start of 'The Adventure of the Speckled Band', for example, both men make light of Watson's rude awakening:

> 'Very sorry to knock you up, Watson,' said he, 'but it's the common lot this morning. Mrs Hudson has been knocked up, she retorted upon me, and I on you.'
> 'What is it, then – a fire?'

Ho, ho. Further proof, for the sceptical teenage reader, of the Victorians' humour bypass. And then the mystery guest arrives seeking Holmes' assistance, which is available to sufficiently interesting potential victims free of charge: 'As to reward, my profession is its own reward.' There is then a chance for Holmes to show off his powers of deduction and tell us something about the visitor before they lay the case before him: 'You have come in by train this morning, I see... I observe the second half of a return ticket in the palm of your left glove.'

By way of introduction, I attempted to organise a mock police identity parade with a Year 9 class who were reading the story. Six volunteers lined up in front of the whiteboard whilst the rest of the class scribbled down Holmes-like deductions based on eagle-eyed observation of their appearance. That was the idea, but as with any activity that relies on pupil input, the results depend on the class in front of you. This particular class spotted another opening in this activity for insulting each other and came up with deductions like: 'boy 1 looks weak', 'boy 4's head is the shape of a melon', 'boy 2 hasn't washed'. I am not convinced that they really understood the notion of deduction. One boy wrote 'boy 3 is tall'.

When the activity descended into farce I retaliated by making them copy out a section of the text containing hidden errors, although my original plan had just been for them to circle the mistakes they could find on the sheet. Copying out may be fairly pointless, but has a valuable calming effect, and many pupils seem to prefer it to creative thought. 'You can't go to break until it's done' also has a pleasing absence of ambiguity which pupils respect.

Another challenge for students in their stories is to modulate between Holmes' steely voice – with its clarity and certainty, born of empire and a superb intellect –

and the outlandish events, sometimes nearly Gothic in their extravagance, with which he deals so squarely. The Gothic lead in *The Adventure of the Speckled Band* falls, predictably, to the only female character – Helen Stoner, who fears she will go the same way as her sister, who died in mysterious circumstances two years earlier: 'It is not cold which makes me shiver... It is fear, Mr Holmes. It is terror.' Holmes' interest is sufficiently roused to give her 'one of his quick, all-comprehensive glances', before patting her arm and saying 'soothingly': 'We shall soon set matters right.'

Her account of the background to the case mixes fantasy with more sturdy, recognisably English elements. Having been born into aristocratic poverty, her stepfather, Dr Grimesby Roylott – the chief suspect in this case – then recovered his fortune in Calcutta, only to lose it again, and his liberty, for beating his 'native butler to death'. Back at the dilapidated family seat in Surrey he engages in a 'series of disgraceful brawls' and reportedly 'hurled the local blacksmith over a parapet into a stream' only the previous week. He also keeps a cheetah and a baboon. During this period, he also found time to marry 'the young widow of Major-General Stoner, of the Bengal Artillery' and lose his wife 'in a railway accident near Crewe'. We are also introduced to Helen Stoner's aunt – a 'Miss Honoria Westphail, who lives near Harrow'.

When urged to employ language devices in their

recreations, boys in Year 9 invariably turned to the simile. One described Holmes getting out of a cramped hackney carriage as 'like a brand new foetus leaving the womb'. The wild animals kept by Dr Roylott also seemed to have an influence on their choice of imagery. Dr Watson, one boy wrote, 'jumped out of the train like a kangaroo'. More poignant, but also slightly at odds with this, was his description of Watson 'huffing and puffing like a dying panda' on account of his old war wound from his time in Afghanistan.

This class were also encouraged to model their victims on the Stoner sisters in the sense of there being two or three of a type – characters who would fit the Victorian setting. Some of the boys got the idea and came up with things like three chimney sweeps or two chambermaids, or a chorus of singers, but one first draft also proposed to kill off a Page 3 Girl and, in another story, a team of BA air stewards came to a sticky end.

At some point their stories need to shift from 221b Baker Street to the crime scene. This usually involves a ride in a hackney carriage and a London train station – Waterloo in the case of 'The Adventure of the Speckled Band'. Despite planning an overnight stay in Surrey – 'Holmes and I had no difficulty in engaging a bedroom and sitting room at the Crown Inn' – there's no evidence of any luggage or an overnight bag. Watson's 'Eley's number two' revolver 'and a toothbrush' are all they'll need, according to Holmes.

From Leatherhead Station there is another trap ride 'through lovely Surrey lanes' before the mood darkens with their arrival at Dr Roylott's run-down mansion, Stoke Moran. Conveniently the owner is out during the afternoon, allowing Holmes to carry out a close inspection of the house and grounds. This includes the doctor's private chamber, which contains a 'large iron safe'. At this point the conversation takes a strange turn. Holmes, apparently rather randomly, asks, 'There isn't a cat in it, for example?'

To which Miss Stoner replies, 'No; we don't keep a cat. But there is a cheetah and a baboon.'

After enjoying a 'quiet pipe' together back at the inn Holmes and Watson then return at night for the climax of the story – the presumed attempt on Miss Stoner's life. As they are crossing the lawn they encounter 'what seemed to be a hideous and distorted child' which jumps out 'from a clump of laurel bushes'. Holmes' 'agitation' almost instantly gives way to a 'low laugh' as he informs Watson: 'That is the baboon.'

Inside Miss Stoner's room – modesty dictates that she withdraws to her old room – they endure what Watson describes as a 'dreadful vigil' sitting in the dark, waiting for Dr Roylott to make his move. Having impressed on Watson the need for absolute silence – 'The least sound would be fatal to our plans' – rather surprisingly, Holmes then starts shouting the minute he sees the assailant, a 'swamp adder': 'You see it, Watson?'

he yelled. 'You see it?' Somehow this doesn't alert Dr Roylott that they're on to him, even though he's in the next room and there is a ventilator connecting the two rooms. Sound may not travel through the opening but the snake retreats from the lash of Holmes' cane through the ventilator in record time, and, with its 'snakish temper' roused, 'flew upon the first person it saw', Dr Roylott, who lets out a 'most horrible cry'.

In the next-door room they are met with 'a singular sight' – Dr Roylott in his dressing gown and 'red heelless Turkish slippers', further proof, presumably, for Victorian readers of his low character. And coiled round his head is 'The band! The speckled band!', or what Watson calls 'a loathsome serpent'.

With the case solved, their last job is to convey Miss Stoner 'by the morning train to the care of her good aunt at Harrow'.

Chapter Seven

Journey's End

Pupils' grasp of time and age is sometimes erratic to say the least. When I was in my forties, pupils guessing my age offered suggestions in the thirties, forties, fifties and even sixties. And they can be similarly sketchy in relation to big historical events, even the two World Wars. I once began a scheme of work on World War One (the play *Journey's End* plus some Wilfred Owen) with a photographed extract from my grandfather's diary – the two weeks leading up to the signing of the armistice on the 11 November. He simply recorded: '11 a.m. hostilities ceased'. Apart from mentioning a change of billet, the only other word he wrote was 'bath' – twice. One for each week. Why would he bother to record this, I asked the class. So deeply impressed on their collective consciousness was their History teacher's account of the Nazi concentration camps, that the class immediately connected my grandfather's weekly bath in 1918 with the fake showers in the gas chambers of Auschwitz. When someone else mentioned

Hitler by way of explanation I realised it was time to abandon historical context and got on with reading the play.

There is a certain inevitability about studying the poems of Wilfred Owen at some point in your time at secondary school. Despite the beauty and power of the poetry, this doesn't always feel like a profound shared experience. 'Anthem for Doomed Youth' is an unfortunate title for a poem which has often been the vehicle by which generations of school children have been introduced to the slightly pointless twin poetic concepts, assonance and consonance. Owen famously wrote that 'I am not concerned with Poetry. My subject is War and the pity of War', but the conspicuous repetition of vowel and consonant sounds in the opening lines isn't something a conscientious English teacher can ignore:

> What passing-bells for these who die as cattle?
> Only the monstrous anger of the guns.
> Only the stuttering rifles' rapid rattle
> Can patter out their hasty orisons.

Similarly, the slightly confusing, but clearly significant, outbreak of sibilance for the description of gunfire in Owen's poem 'Exposure': 'Sudden successive flights of bullets streak the silence.' The discussion of this doesn't always go to plan. To the question – 'What sort of sound does the letter "s" make? Is it a hard or soft sound?' – the answer has sometimes been 'hard'. This isn't what the teacher is looking for, and requires a stream of softly spoken examples of soft things beginning with 's' to get the discussion back on track.

Shared profound experience isn't really what pupils are looking for from their English lessons, and they are unlikely to admit to it even if it happens – least of all to their teacher. That would just be embarrassing. Fortunately, R C Sherriff's play *Journey's End* keeps a tight lid on emotions and the grisly reality of war, especially at the start, where class reading can enter the realm of slapstick as students are introduced to the full power of the English stiff upper lip. Despite the seriousness of its subject, pupils, boys especially, will find ways to subvert class reading. More confident readers tend to be very hard on classmates who misread a word or get into a muddle, and are always ready to pounce with a chorus of derision. An unfortunate boy in Year 11 read 'bible' with a short 'i' on one occasion – as in Officer Dibble from *Top Cat* – much to the delight of the rest of the class. The first few pages of *Journey's End* contain several potential banana skins for the volunteers reading – lumbago, neuralgia and blancmange – which are also excuses for the rest of the class to take the mick. How students navigate these tricky words can dictate the level of seriousness in the classroom and the sort of group reading that follows. Nor does it help that Mason's (the cook's) 'pink blancmange…ain't anywhere near stiff yet'.

The sharpest and grubbiest minds will probably already have spotted ample opportunity for double entendre well before they meet Mason's limp blancmange, and reading can descend into a *Carry On* film. After introducing his sock to Osborne on page 2 ('It's a nice-looking sock'), Captain Hardy, whose company are being 'relieved' (oh dear), exclaims 'Splendid! You know, I'm awfully glad you've come' – none of which is particularly helpful to the teacher who is trying to keep order. Getting the correct pronunciation for 'blancmange', as with enjambment – another fairly pointless poetic concept pupils have to learn – requires students to put on French accents and this also encourages a rowdy atmosphere.

Secondary schools have become far less homophobic in the last few years, but it is also fair to say that progress is relative, and in the case of boys' schools has been made from a very low level. There are quite a few lines in Act One which had boys at my old school squirming. They didn't really know how to take Osborne's 'I love that fellow' about Stanhope, the young captain of the company, or Hardy's reply – 'Oh, you sweet sentimental old darling.' There was also a certain amount of embarrassment from the boy reading Stanhope at the end of Act One when he asks Osborne (unfortunately being played by me, his teacher) to tuck him up in bed – 'Kiss me, Uncle.'

Despite all of these immature distractions (and also partly because of them) *Journey's End* is a fantastic play to read with a class. The distribution of parts requires some care and sensitivity from the teacher. For example, it is very easy to give the part of Mason, the chirpy cook, to a tough boy with poor grammar and/or a cockney accent. Meanwhile, Raleigh, the new officer straight out of public school, will invariably go to someone (like Raleigh) deemed to be 'keen' – a dubious distinction in a class of teenage boys and avoided at all costs by the majority. Then there is Trotter, described in the stage directions as 'short and fat'. There are numerous follow-up references to his weight and eating, so the teacher has to be careful with who gets the part. And it is best for the teacher to keep the part of Osborne for themselves – the older officer the other men call 'Uncle'.

The real issue for Trotter is not fitting into his trousers ('Lord! I must get my fat down') but fitting in with the other officers – not Hibbert, who is in the same boat as him, but the privately educated, sports-playing triumvirate of Stanhope, Osborne and Raleigh. Osborne has played rugger for England and also Harlequins, and Stanhope, we learn from Raleigh, 'was skipper of Rugger at Barford and kept wicket for the eleven', as well as being a 'jolly good bat'. No man's land is described by Osborne as 'About the breadth of a rugger field.'

The downside of their sporting excellence is that Osborne and Raleigh get selected to lead the raid on Wednesday afternoon at the start of Act Three. (The action of the play begins on Monday evening, and ends on Thursday 'towards dawn'.) Trotter is regarded as too fat to 'make the dash', and so lives to enjoy the special celebratory dinner – 'a fresh chicken... two bottles of champagne and half a dozen cigars' – served on Wednesday evening, despite Osborne's death by hand grenade.

'Poor Osborne!' says the Colonel, who had selected him to lead the raid. Naturally, the Colonel speaks the same language as Stanhope, Osborne and Raleigh, and frames the raid in terms of a training ground move on the rugby pitch: 'Raleigh, just go in like blazes. Grab hold of the first Boche you see and bundle him across here.'

For some reason Osborne takes his school master's whistle with him on the raid and tells Raleigh he will blow it 'now and then to show you where I am', which presumably doesn't help with the element of surprise, or his chances of survival.

The Colonel is less comfortable talking to the ten nameless 'men' going on the raid. 'Are they cheerful?' he asks, incongruously, moments before they make a suicidal daylight raid across no man's land, and has to be leaned on by Stanhope to speak to them:

Stanhope:	Would you like to go up and speak to them, sir?
Colonel:	Well, don't you think they'd rather be left alone?
Stanhope:	I think they would appreciate a word or two.
Colonel:	All right. If you think they would.

Trotter can't transform himself into an accomplished athlete but does what he can to hide the real Trotter, particularly when Mason, the cook, is around, who'd presumably also like to have a go at being an officer, with a servant (like him) and a bed in the dugout. Trotter's first words are: 'Ha! Give me apricots every time! I 'ate pineapple chunks; too bloomin' sickly for me!' But then, as if remembering that he's surrounded by ex-public school boys, he puts on a 'pair of pince-nez from his tunic pocket' and introduces himself to Raleigh like Tarzan talking to Jane in the jungle, before switching to his poshest voice:

Trotter:	You Raleigh?
Raleigh:	Yes.
Pause	
Trotter:	I'm Trotter.
Raleigh:	Oh, yes?
Pause	
Trotter:	How *are* you?

There then follows, in the stage directions, six lines of what every self-respecting GCSE exam text needs – a passage of symbolism for pupils to decode. It describes Trotter's struggle with the box he's sitting on at the dinner table – either too low or too high – and represents the struggle he has for social position and acceptance.

Another rather unsubtle giveaway of Trotter's real self is his advice to Raleigh to wear his gas mask 'sort of tucked up under your chin like a serviette'. This leads naturally in class discussion to the obvious 'How posh are you?' question – napkin or serviette? In fact, I suspect, the majority of pupils just guess, and tend to look blank at the mention of either napkin or serviette.

Although he's a relatively peripheral figure, Mason – the underdog/dogsbody in the dugout – tends to be students' favourite character, but this doesn't mean that they, or their teacher, were prepared for an exam question on him, which is what our exam board set one year. Teachers have now been barred from visiting the exam room to have a quick peep at the question. But this was before the new ruling and I looked up from the exam paper on this occasion to see rows of accusatory looks from the massed ranks in the sports hall, as they took in the fact that the character question was on Mason, the cook, about whom they knew nothing beyond his 'limp blancmange' and onion tea.

Raleigh, and his letter home to Mama and Papa,

has usually been the focus of the creative writing task for pupils studying the play in Year 9. Invariably this comes back browned with tea or coffee stains and baked in the oven to give it the appearance of antiquity, a presentational device some younger pupils are inclined to use for every piece of homework, whatever the task. For students who have left their letter in the oven for too long, this is like handling ancient parchment or an extremely thin poppadom, and the challenge is to return their homework in one piece.

Like *Of Mice and Men*, *Journey's End* was dropped from the current Govian GCSE English Literature specification, and both texts have now been shunted into Year 9, which was where I taught it most recently at the high-achieving girls' state school. There was very little enthusiasm for the play from the girls in my class, and none of the frivolity which had enlivened the reading with groups of naughty boys. 'Stakeholders' is a word that has crept into the vocabulary of Senior Leadership Teams in schools, and, on reflection, it is likely that these Year 9 girls felt very little stake in this particular text. Having devoted the half-term before Christmas to *Of Mice and Men*, a novel seriously lacking in female representation, they then went straight into the work of another male writer in which there are no female characters, and very few mentions of any female. Trotter's wife writes to him to ask if he has fleas, and Osborne's wife sends him a 'packet of

Lux', a cleaning product. There is also a discussion of Hibbert's dirty postcards during the drunken dinner in Act Three, featuring phrases like 'There's a nice pair of legs for you' and 'Glorious bedroom eyes', so it's not all that surprising if a class of girls decides this is not the text for them.

Girls in this school used the expression 'drama' to describe even the most petty and minor disagreements between them, and must have found Osborne, in particular (like Mr Darcy), a rather cold fish, and his emotional control off the scale. Informed that he will be leading the suicidal raid across no man's land, Osborne simply responds with, 'Oh. I see.' He then reassures Stanhope that there are no hard feelings with, 'That's all right, old chap.' Not an expression I can imagine hearing from the young men with six packs and flip-flops on *Love Island*, the girls' favourite TV programme.

There is an outbreak of touchy-feeliness right at the end of the play as Raleigh lies dying on Osborne's bed in the officer's dugout. Stanhope nurses him through his final moments – 'He bathes the boy's face' – and there is a moving reconciliation involving first names:

Raleigh: Hullo – Dennis –
Stanhope: Well, Jimmy – you got one quickly.

But there is no lowering or relaxing of their stiff upper lips. Raleigh has been hit in the back by a shell at the start of the big German attack. The situation, we know, is fairly desperate but according to Stanhope the German guns are just 'making a bit of a row'. Stanhope may be every inch the public school educated officer but he hasn't previously spoken like a parody of one, which is what he does now as a comfort for his protégé from their school days – 'Steady, old boy' and 'Yes, old boy' and 'It's all right, old chap.' This sort of talk comes more naturally to Raleigh – only recently out of school – who, even as he lies dying, doesn't forget the importance of being a team player: 'It's awfully decent of you to bother, Dennis. I feel rotten lying here – everybody else – up there.' And then, 'I say, Dennis, don't you wait – if – if you want to be getting on.'

Raleigh takes his last breath with 'something between a sob and a moan' and a 'solitary candle-flame' illuminates Stanhope, the last one standing of the public school, sports playing officers. A message from Trotter, the common man, summons Stanhope from the dugout to join his men, just in time. A shell falls with a 'shriek and bursts on the dugout roof' and the 'timber props'/posh officer class fall. 'The play ends.'

Chapter Eight

Brighton Rock

At some point in the third year (Year 9) my old English class started reading Graham Greene's novel *Brighton Rock* with Mr Tooth. Only Pinkie Brown's name survived in my memory across the thirty years before I read it again, properly, in preparation for teaching it to Year 10. Pinkie is a seventeen-year-old gang member/aspiring gang leader, who murders a man with a stick of rock at the end of Chapter One and spends the rest of the novel trying to cover his tracks. This includes the rather desperate measure of marrying Rose, the only witness who can contradict the timings in his alibi – something not then permitted in English Law from a spouse. Marriage to Rose is clearly not something Pinkie relishes and there are a number of fairly unsubtle clues which point to his true sexuality, his name being perhaps the most obvious. Had we got that far in the story and managed to pick up on these clues, it would have made for an interesting discussion given Mr Tooth's avoidance of all things sexual. He was a devout Christian and when confronted in a text by sexual content, invariably hid behind the phrase 'to lie with', as in 'The poet wants her to lie with him.' By the time we reached the sixth form this produced knowing smiles and someone would ask, 'What do you mean, *lie with*, sir?'

Whether it was the prospect of this embarrassing conversation that prompted Mr Tooth to abandon the novel, unfinished, I don't know. He was a young and inexperienced teacher, and may simply have launched into a new text because he thought it would get him to half-term, and there were enough copies in the stock cupboard. This is an easy mistake to make and there is nothing worse than the sinking sensation you get as you realise you're stuck with a text the class have no interest in. Sometimes this can even extend to the film version of the novel you have rashly started, by which time you know you're really in trouble.

After my first year of teaching in a boys' comprehensive school, I foolishly asked the Head of Department if I could keep my Year 9 class and take them through their GCSE. I have no idea why I opted for this course of self-harm; instead of being able to make a fresh start on the back of a year's hard-won experience and assert myself with boys who hadn't witnessed the various sticky moments and humiliating climbdowns of the first year, I chose to jump straight back into the frying pan. At some point in Year 10, after several particularly aimless lessons, I attempted yet another reset/relaunch by giving each boy a copy of George Orwell's *1984*. A heavyweight tome would be just the thing to win back waning respect, I reasoned. There was also a film version and the department had it on video.

Unfortunately, I had forgotten that large sections of the text are virtually impossible to read aloud, and completely failed to anticipate that they would have zero interest in the Cold War, communist totalitarian stuff that I had found so appealing at school. The result was that I don't think we even finished the film. The following week I drew a veil over yet another doomed educational experiment and started on something else, prompting disgruntled questions along the lines of, 'What was the point of watching that film last week, sir?'

The most recent film version of *Brighton Rock*, which is reimagined in the 1960s with Pinkie as a scooter driving mod, was more popular than the film of *1984*, but the text proved to be just as inaccessible and my Year 10 classes never got beyond the end of Chapter One. Some of the confusion is clearly deliberate on Greene's part, but that counts for nothing with groups of impatient fifteen-year-old boys. A man, identified in the first line as Hale, knows he is a marked man. We aren't told why, or why, in the circumstances, he is still walking round Brighton leaving prize cards for a national newspaper as his alter ego Kolley Kibber. Or why, when he stops in a pub for a glass of gin, he is addressed as Fred. At least Hale shares our confusion and replies with, 'Who are you Freding? I'm not Fred.' In fact, his Christian name is Charles, which Hale reveals later in the chapter, whilst also admitting to the reader that he does use Fred 'to chance acquaintances'.

The 'boy of about seventeen' doing the Freding is the central character Pinkie Brown, but has yet to be introduced, which doesn't help either. My attempt to clear up the confusion via the two film versions just made matters worse. Having made a big thing about the title and Pinkie's stick of rock as the murder weapon, the modern film version shows him murdering Hale with a large pebble, and, in the old black and white film, he seems to be pushed from a ghost train on the pier. This all just confused the class further and prompted a stream of frustrated questions ('So who's that?') and complaints ('I don't get this! Sir, this is moist').

Chapter One contains a number of classic Graham Greeneisms but they fell on stony ground in the case of the difficult class of Year 10 boys. Pinkie's 'grey eyes' are described as having 'an effect of heartlessness like an old man's in which human feeling has died'. The face has a 'starved intensity' which exhibits 'a kind of hideous and unnatural pride'. When pressed for comment on the characterisation the only opinion offered by a boy on the back row was a weary sigh and an 'It's long, sir.'

This class took rather more notice of the many references to Ida Arnold's 'big breasts', perhaps like Hale, clinging to them as the one subject in Chapter One not shrouded in ambiguity. They are also described as 'great' and 'magnificent', and, when Hale is next to her in the back of the taxi, become 'her great open friendly breasts'.

Hale's, and my class's, breast fixation ('You thought of sucking babies when you looked at her') could be another reason why the novel has fallen out of favour as a GCSE set text. Notwithstanding Ida's strength of character the representation of female characters is not much more enlightened than it is in *Of Mice and Men* or any more inspiring for a class of teenage girls. And, as with Curley's wife, physical properties are the defining features: all along the seafront girls sit in deckchairs 'waiting to be picked...clerks, shop-girls, hairdressers – you could pick out the hairdressers by their new and daring perms...' Hale is desperately seeking the protection of a companion but the girls 'stared at him like duchesses with large cold eyes'. In the end he sits down next to a 'fat spotty creature in pink whose feet hardly touched the ground'. After a page and a half of being identified as 'the fat girl' we learn that this is Molly, and her friend – 'the pasty girl' – is Delia, which perhaps represents a small advance on Curley's nameless wife.

Towards the end of the film the Catholic subtheme

starts to intrude and confused things even further with the class of difficult Year 10 boys. In one scene, Rose is seen praying anxiously to a figure of Christ on the cross. Up to this point there had only been little hints of Rose and Pinkie's shared Catholicism, so I thought it necessary to stop the film and mention it. As usual I had failed to anticipate what was puzzling them. The only question that came back was an apparently serious enquiry about the figure of Christ: 'Sir, has he got a six pack?'

Chapter Nine

Frankenstein

After a few days of searing heat and then several weeks of torrential downpours, the school holidays are over and schools are finally reopening thanks to various coronavirus protocols and the introduction of so-called 'Year Bubbles'. The first two days at my latest school were mainly spent in the sports hall, sat two metres apart from my new colleagues, whilst members of the Senior Leadership Team went over the arrangements they have put in place to keep us all safe.

For my first lesson this morning with Year 9, I resurrected a favourite one-off lesson on an extract from *Decline and Fall* by Evelyn Waugh – the section where the hapless hero, Paul Pennyfeather, teaches his first lesson. The first slide of my PowerPoint set the scene as Pennyfeather – 'dumb with terror' – confronts his class after morning assembly: 'Ten boys sat before him, their hands folded, their eyes bright with expectation.'

I asked the class what stood out as being odd in this sentence, expecting them to comment on the extremely small class size, which in the past had led to a confusing discussion of the difference between private and public schools. But this morning a girl offered something I hadn't heard before – the strange thing, she said, is that the boys are 'bright with expectation'. A rather sad statement from one so young, but perhaps understandable given the last six months. Sadly, the new COVID-related restrictions will make it even harder to brighten a student's day – strict seating plans, no movement around the room, no group work, no drama, no fun or games of any sort.

The past, however, as well-read students and teachers of English Literature know, is a 'foreign country'/another kettle of fish, where things are done very differently; and so it was that one afternoon, towards the end of the 1990s, the class of Year 10 boys, with whom I had been reading *Decline and Fall*, filmed a spirited reconstruction of the opening scene, in which Paul Pennyfeather is set upon by a drunken mob – the members of a posh drinking club, who are on the rampage in Scone College. They take exception to Paul's tie, because of its similarity to their own club tie, and retaliate by removing most of his clothes. Our version simply required the boy playing the part of Pennyfeather to wear his football shorts under his trousers in preparation for his debagging and subsequent dash to safety, all of which was to be filmed covertly from an upper window on an old VHS video camera. The nearest thing we had to the grassy quadrangle of an Oxford College was the square rose garden on the old side of the school, enclosed by three, unfortunately, not four walls, which meant that the scene was also witnessed by bemused members of the public walking past the school on their way to and from town.

Looking back now, I can't account for this particular lesson plan, or why I thought it would be a good idea to let another class – the difficult class of Year 10 boys – go out into the school playground to play a game of cricket, one morning towards the end of the summer term. The tenuous English teaching connection/excuse was that they had been working on a short story called 'The Red Ball' by the Trinidadian writer Ismith Khan. Fortunately, the two most difficult members of the class were missing for the big match, and we managed to decamp from their classroom to the playground without a major incident. I had again failed to anticipate the interest of members of the public, who kept stopping to watch the game from the other side of the playground fence, and from where they could also hear the constant stream of abuse being exchanged on the field of play. This was hardly a great advert for the school, so I did my best to contain it by moving antagonistic members of the fielding team as far away from each other as possible. But when the non-striking batsman berated the bowler for being too fat at the top of his voice, I thought I had no choice but to make an example of him in front of the watching public and so terminated his innings and sent him back to his teammates waiting under the tree, where he sat sulking and swearing in full view.

Back in the COVID-19 present, my drive to work, along a very straight A road, seems spookily in tune with this rather dull new reality. At one point, where the road is fringed on either side by fields, a line from another Evelyn Waugh novel comes to me – the 'dun ploughland' we see out of Brenda Last's window in *A Handful of Dust* as she takes in the death of her only child, John Andrew. The pang of regret that follows this recollection is not out of sympathy with Brenda (earlier she lets slip 'Thank God' when she realises that the fatality involves her son John Andrew, not her lover John Beaver) but a painful reminder of another teaching fiasco.

Towards the end of the last week of the autumn term, about a dozen years ago, a very clever and conscientious boy in the upper sixth came to talk to me about resitting his English Literature AS level – the half course he had completed the previous summer. He had achieved a very creditable B grade, and then dropped English Literature because it was his weakest subject and he was intending to pursue a career in dentistry. But such was the competition for university places, he had now decided that his B grade wouldn't look good on his UCAS application, and that the only solution was to retake in January and get an A. He had been going over the A level syllabus, he told me during morning registration. Did I realise, he asked very politely, that the novel I had been studying since September with the lower sixth was no longer on the list of set texts. The specification had changed for the new academic year.

The novel in question was *A Handful of Dust* – aptly titled considering what my Year 12 class were left with after three and a half months of close study. The room swam before me and I had to sit down. A moment later, I ran off in a panic to find my copy of the syllabus. He was right. Blinded by my enthusiasm for what is one of my favourite novels, I had been teaching them a text which wouldn't be on the exam paper in June.

Pleading phone calls to the exam board achieved nothing; there was still time, they said, to cover one of the novels that was on the specification. The choice of new text from the revised list came down to a shoot-out between *The Picture of Dorian Gray* by Oscar Wilde, or Mary Shelley's *Frankenstein*, a novel I had read before, many moons ago, and disliked. I immediately ordered a class set of *Dorian Gray* and settled down to reading it over the Christmas holiday. After about fifty pages – as far as I got – it became obvious that this was the wrong choice. I couldn't imagine any of this particular group of boys getting even that far or talking to them about the decadent movement. I also didn't have a clue how I'd go about teaching it.

I left it until January to break the news of my incompetence to the class, accompanied on the same day by a grovelling letter home to their parents. Fortunately, we already had some old copies of *Frankenstein* in the stock cupboard and there was no time to waste.

After closer inspection, the novel turns out, appropriately, to be a fairly scathing attack on male stupidity, and provides some much needed levelling up after all the unsatisfactory characterisation of the women in other set texts. Not that the female characters get to branch out or do anything very interesting. Quite the reverse. Victor Frankenstein's mother Caroline is singled out for her 'soft and benevolent mind', and that is the blueprint for the other female characters. Having been born into wealth, her father, previously a prosperous merchant, falls into debt and depression. Caroline attends him 'with the greatest tenderness', until she is discovered by Victor's father Alphonse kneeling by his coffin 'weeping bitterly': 'Two years after this event Caroline became his wife.'

Alphonse has much more emotional intelligence than his son Victor – who appears to have none – and proves an excellent husband, if in a rather old-fashioned way: 'He strove to shelter her, as a fair exotic is sheltered by the gardener, from every rough wind...'

Like a Swiss First Lady, or Miss World contestant, Caroline enjoys visiting 'the cottages of the poor', even whilst on holiday, and returns from a trip to Italy with an adopted sister for Victor – Elizabeth. Even though she is discovered living in a 'poor cot', cared for by 'a peasant and his wife', Elizabeth is clearly not meant for a life of poverty. The other children are 'dark-eyed, hardy little vagrants' but she appears 'of a different stock' – and, like her new mother, is described with gentler garden imagery: 'a garden rose among dark-leaved brambles'.

Elizabeth's choices later on don't exactly break the mould or ruffle the feathers of her male companions, Victor and his close friend Henry Clerval. She keeps herself busy with romantic poetry, in admiring 'the majestic and wondrous scenes which surrounded our Swiss home', and in teaching the boys how to be kinder: 'The saintly soul of Elizabeth shone like a shrine-dedicated lamp in our peaceful home. Her sympathy was ours, her smile, her soft voice, the sweet glance of her celestial eyes, were ever there to bless and animate us.'

Despite this guiding light, Victor still manages to make a horrible mess of everything, although he isn't the first self-centred, egotistical rich boy we encounter. The novel begins with Captain Walton's letters home to his sister, Margaret Saville, who, from the look of things, is another long suffering, stay at home female character. Walton has bigger fish to fry than his sister – discovering a new passage through the North Pole and the 'wondrous power which attracts the [compass] needle' – but still expects her to keep writing to him at 'every opportunity': 'I may receive your letters on some occasions when I need them most to support my spirits.'

'I have no friend,' he complains to Margaret, who must be tempted to write back and ask why, in that case, he is sailing to somewhere as uninhabited as the North Pole. She could also point out that beggars can't be choosers and that he might set the bar a bit lower for his 'special friend' profile: 'gentle yet courageous, possessed of a cultivated as well as of a capacious mind, whose tastes are like my own' etc. In Victor, Walton has met someone just as inattentive to his family as he is to poor Margaret. Professor Marilyn Butler calls *Frankenstein* a comic 'portrayal of male inattentiveness', although it's not very funny for his father, Alphonse, or his adopted sister, Elizabeth, who have just lost a much loved wife and mother (Caroline dies in Chapter Three, shortly before Victor enrols at the University of Ingolstadt). Consumed by what he calls 'natural philosophy' (basically science), Victor acknowledges that 'Two years passed...during which I paid no visit to Geneva' (home).

The creature (pupils have to be reminded not

to refer to it as the monster) is on the receiving end of even shabbier treatment. Having been stitched together from spare body parts collected from graves and charnel houses, Victor hasn't given the creature a very good start in life as it is. Prior to animation, and presumably anticipating the first of many designer babies, Victor seems very excited by the prospect of becoming a parent: 'A new species would bless me as its creator and source; many happy and excellent natures would owe their being to me.' The reality of the creature he has made ('this catastrophe') comes as a very nasty shock to Victor, who, typically, frames the disappointment in terms of his own needs – 'For this I had deprived myself of rest and health' – and goes straight to bed without bothering to undress. Shortly after he falls into a nervous fever – 'which confined me for several months' – but is nursed back to health by the ever reliable Clerval. The creature, meanwhile, is left to fend for itself, and for the moment vanishes from view.

Despite the considerable anxiety his family have suffered on his behalf, Victor's return to Geneva has to wait until the following autumn. It is then further delayed and postponed until May. And then when Clerval proposes 'a pedestrian tour in the environs of Ingolstadt' Victor goes off walking and delays for another two weeks.

The feel-good factor from the fortnight spent 'in

these perambulations' is shattered by a letter from his father, informing Victor of the death of his little brother William, and urging his immediate return. Perhaps starting to sense that this might be a mess of his making – 'a thousand nameless evils that made me tremble' – Victor drags his feet for two days 'at Lausanne', and then arrives back in Geneva so late that the city gates are locked and he is 'obliged to pass the night at Secheron, a village at the distance of half a league from the city'.

When he does finally arrive home it is to find that their servant, Justine Moritz, is being tried on that day for William's murder. Having seen the creature the previous evening, stealing 'from behind a clump of trees', Victor knows she's not the murderer and pledges, via a slightly confusing conditional phrase, that 'A thousand times rather would I have confessed myself guilty of the crime' – but in the end says nothing at the trial. Elizabeth speaks movingly on her behalf but Justine is condemned. Most of the emotional commentary is (self) centred on Victor: 'My own agitation and anguish was extreme during the whole trial.' Particularly insensitive, even by Victor's high standards, is his presumption that 'The torture of the accused' – Justine is hung 'on the morrow' – 'did not equal mine', to which one boy responded with a heartfelt 'That's well out of order!'

Alphonse should really know better than to warn

a Gothic figure like his son against 'an appearance of immoderate grief'. And the remarks that follow, about 'the discharge of duty' and being 'fit for society', are also wasted on Victor, whose immediate response is to keep to himself, first by rowing out to the middle of Lake Geneva, and then by means of a walking trip towards Chamonix. Having given the rest of his family the slip he can now receive the 'consolation' that 'these sublime and magnificent scenes afforded'. This is the basic thematic structure that my hard-pressed and slightly resentful A level students spent much of the spring term furnishing with supportive quotations: the social benevolence and engagement of his father and Elizabeth, and various other good characters, versus Victor's social disengagement, or withdrawal.

Because this was an A level group, the job of reading it was for them to complete at home. Having eaten humble pie and apologised profusely, my letter to the parents went on to beg their assistance in this regard, and rather hopefully included a date (I think a fortnight away) by which students should have read what is a relatively short book. Later, after they'd sat their final exam, quite a few of the boys in the class admitted that they had barely read any of it, but had relied instead on my 'run-through' in lessons and an audio book version. But in terms of keeping the workload to a minimum, we landed on our feet with *Frankenstein*. The simple two-sided thematic scheme – the creature's side and Victor's side, or social benevolence versus social withdrawal – is more the sort of thing you expect from a GCSE text, which is what it has since become.

Nowhere is this more apparent in the pair's language (Assessment Objective 2) than during their bad-tempered encounter high up in the Alps. It isn't clear how much effort it costs Victor to get to the top of Montanvert, or if his elation at reaching the summit ('My heart...now swelled with something like joy') is an effect of the exertion of the climb, or just the view – probably the latter given what he says at the start of Chapter Ten: 'My mule was brought to the door, and I resolved to ascend to the summit of Montanvert.' But having managed to escape 'from all littleness of feeling' (difficult matters like his grieving family) and arrive at the 'glittering pinnacle' – even if it is by mule power – who should he bump into but the 'wretch whom I had created'. Victor doesn't hold back. Having got over the compulsory spasm of Gothic trembling, Victor recovers to 'overwhelm him with words expressive of furious detestation and contempt'. 'Begone, vile insect! or rather, stay, that I may trample you to dust!' Victor yells, forgetting that the creature is twice his size.

The creature's measured reply – 'I expected this reception' – is more Mr Knightley ('a sensible man about seven or eight-and-thirty'), or Mr Darcy, than 'Abhorred monster!' And like Jane Austen's sensible male leads his theme is 'duty': 'Do your duty towards me, and I will do mine towards you and the rest of mankind.' Victor isn't listening and tries to fight him – 'I sprang on him' – but is 'easily eluded' and told to calm down so that the creature can tell his story.

It isn't one that students find particularly engaging. Girls at the high-achieving girls' state school, who had some affinity with Gothic sensibility, found the creature rather a dry stick for their taste. Scary stories and the supernatural (as long as they were their scary stories) were the one thing they were enthusiastic about. On one occasion, when half the class were missing on a Geography trip, they asked me if they could turn the lights off and tell scary stories. Sensing an easy lesson, I let two of the leading voices in the class take charge, and sat at the back whilst they shared dark tales from sleepovers, or worse still, being home alone. Unfortunately for them, the creature's voice (or 'address' as it would be described in a Jane Austen novel) is more Mr Darcy than Count Dracula. Despite his lack of formal education, and spending his formative years in a small shed, the creature speaks like a gentleman from the Age of Reason.

There is a 'small and almost imperceptible chink' into the cottage to which the shed is attached, allowing the creature to observe the comings and goings and social interaction of its inhabitants, the De Lacey family. By happy coincidence, an exotic stranger comes to stay, who can barely speak a word of their (unspecified) language and requires daily language lessons. This is Safie, girlfriend of Felix De Lacey, who is introduced as 'his sweet Arabian'. By means of remote learning through the chink in the wall the creature makes startling progress and can boast 'I improved more rapidly than the Arabian, who understood very little'.

By further happy coincidence, the creature, whilst walking in the woods, stumbles on a 'leathern portmanteau' containing a number of key texts – 'Paradise Lost, a volume of Plutarch's Lives, and The Sorrows of Werter.' – and his education is soon complete. But for all his learning, the creature isn't the raciest storyteller, favouring instead a flat neo-classical style in his accounts of cottage life:

> Soon after this the young man returned, bearing on his shoulders a load of wood. The girl met him at the door, helped to relieve him of his burden, and, taking some of the fuel into the cottage, placed it on the fire; then she and the youth went apart into a nook of the cottage, and he showed her a large loaf and a piece of cheese. She seemed pleased, and went into the garden for some roots and plants...

There is absolutely no mileage in asking students to recreate the creature's steady voice. Instead, pupils in the lower years are often asked to model their Gothic recreation on Frankenstein's tremulous account of the November night on which the creature is sparked into life – and to imitate a style that even the author, Mary Shelley, clearly thinks is ridiculous, if her treatment of Victor is anything to go by.

At one point in the Year 9 scheme of work for this term, this moment in *Frankenstein* is paired with the troll from the first Harry Potter novel – the bit where Harry and Ron find it in the girls' toilets with Hermione. Having introduced the class to the standard Gothic ingredients in our first lesson, via the passage from *Frankenstein*, in the next lesson we looked at how J K Rowling adapts these conventions with the troll – fusing scary monster with more endearingly friendly features – before they set about creating their own hybrid creature. To assist the creative process, and as it was Friday afternoon, I also asked them to draw their monster. This took up most of the lesson but didn't necessarily provide the basis for a serious attempt at Gothic fiction. One girl simply drew one of the Teletubbies, holding a bloody dagger in each blobby paw. In fact, most of their drawings seemed to be modelled on cartoon characters from children's TV with the addition of various bloodstained weapons.

After the relative sanity of the creature's story, the novel lurches back into Gothic madness with Victor agreeing to the creature's parting request – the creation of 'one as deformed and horrible as myself' to be his companion. Victor decides to relocate to England for this purpose, where, he says, there were 'philosophers...whose knowledge and discoveries were of indispensable use to me in my present undertaking' – as if the scientific community in England had made a specialism of hideous monster brides. Ever sociable, Victor leaves Henry behind in Perth, and sets up his laboratory in a deserted spot in 'one of the remotest of the Orkneys': 'On the whole island there were but three miserable huts, and one of these was vacant when I arrived. This I hired.'

Here he toils, until being visited one evening by the creature he is provoked into a change of heart and destroys the prototype she-monster/creature he has been working on. Despite this setback, the creature still manages to sound like an enraged Mr Darcy – 'Slave, I before reasoned with you, but you have proved yourself unworthy of my condescension' – before stomping off with a parting shot about being with Victor on his wedding night.

Victor's next job is to pack the 'remains of the half-finished creature' into a basket, concealed under a layer of stones, and row out to sea and throw them overboard. Somehow Victor can't even manage to do this without over-egging the situation. Refreshed by a stiff 'north-east breeze' he prolongs his 'stay on the water', and promptly falls asleep. When he wakes up an even stiffer wind is propelling him towards the coast of Ireland, where, on landing, he is dragged off to see the magistrate and placed under suspicion for the murder of Henry Clerval.

Instead of meeting Victor in Perth, as he proposes in his final letter, Henry has presumably encountered the furious creature, and paid the price for Victor's decision to down tools. When shown his friend's corpse, Victor collapses with yet more 'strong convulsions', and then comes down with another fever, and spends two months 'on the point of death' raving like a madman.

Once again everyone else rallies round Victor. The helpful magistrate contacts his father. Alphonse travels to Ireland and arranges their return to Geneva, and Elizabeth writes with a proposal of marriage, the effect of which is not to start Victor's heart racing in her direction, but to resurrect the creature's threat about being with him on his wedding night. Victor's attitude seems to be that if it's coming, he might as well get it over with as soon as possible – 'Well, be it so; a deadly struggle would then assuredly take place' – but at no point does it occur to him to warn Elizabeth of the danger they might be in.

Victor's indifference to his own survival is usually shared by students by the time they reach this point ('This is well boring, sir!'), and they tend to react to his wedding night antics with amused resignation. Whilst he's doing his Inspector Clouseau impression, 'walking up and down the passages of the house, and inspecting every corner that might afford a retreat to my adversary', Elizabeth is left to her own devices, until visited by the creature, who strangles her. Victor is summoned by 'a dreadful scream', but it's too late.

What follows is a race to the North Pole as Victor pursues the creature to the ends of the earth, bent on retribution – what Marilyn Butler calls 'a blackly funny homoerotic mime' in which the 'three male narrators pair off in every combination'. When Victor eventually runs out of steam, Walton is on hand to be his new best friend – to listen to his story, massage Victor's ego in his final hours, and write it all down in a bumper-sized letter to his sister Margaret.

Chapter Ten

Romeo and Juliet

Some good news today, or at least what I thought was some good news for my Year 11 classes. They can forget about *A Christmas Carol* – it won't be one of their exam texts. It had been expected that next summer's slimmed down final exam would be without the poetry just for this year, which would save the most work and so be the most popular option with students and teachers. For that reason alone, it probably hasn't been allowed to happen. Having spent the best part of a term going through *A Christmas Carol*, the Year 11 class I spoke to this morning didn't think this was such good news, and on reflection I can see their point – they have already lost more than a term of school to the lockdown, and this would effectively mean that they lost another one.

With Michael Gove still in the government it was never going to be an option to drop the Shakespeare text. Without a department of his own, the Chancellor of the Duchy of Lancaster presumably still has time to check the current Education Secretary's homework, that's if Gavin Williamson ever does it. So with what feels like inevitability, the academic year is starting with *Romeo and Juliet* – selected extracts from Shakespeare's play and all of Baz Luhrmann's modern film version. Heeding the advice of SLT (Senior Leadership Team), one of my new colleagues attempted to recap on what the students had learned during lockdown (by watching Baz Luhrmann's film). What are the 'two households' who are 'alike in dignity' called, he asked the class, to which someone replied, without any trace of irony, 'Montagues and DiCaprios'. Leonardo DiCaprio, who plays Romeo, is the main talking point amongst the girls in my class, causing yet another structural divide: fans of his puppyish good looks and those who aren't.

Whatever their teacher might be thinking as they launch into *Romeo and Juliet* or *Macbeth* yet again, pupils tend to have a grudging respect for Shakespeare and seem to recognise instinctively that they are taking part in a non-negotiable rite of passage. There may also be some satisfaction at doing something which is supposed to be difficult, and about which they can groan to their younger siblings who do easier stuff in the lower years or at primary school.

This was the spirit in which I approached *Macbeth* in 1982 when I was in the fourth year (Year 10). By then Roman Polanski's film version was already more than ten years old and showing its age. Our English teachers arranged a trip to the cinema to see a special screening of the film for local schools. When we got back to school we were subjected to a furious post-mortem about our behaviour, conducted by our Year Head, who also happened to be our English teacher. The first sighting of the three witches at the start of the film had been greeted with an outbreak of 'That's your mum', and at the end, when Macbeth's decapitated head is waved around on the end of a pike staff, somebody from our group shouted out, 'He was game for a laugh!' – a reference to a popular Saturday-night light entertainment show.

Pupils today are still using Polanski's 1971 film in their English lessons, and giggling when 'Playboy Productions' appears in the credits, and at the cheap special effects for Macbeth's 'dagger of the mind', at the naked witches in Act Four (still somebody's 'mum'), and at the stiff finale – the showdown between Macbeth and Macduff.

The fight scene at the end is a particular challenge for school productions, lacking any special effects or expertise in stage fighting. During one school production, as Macbeth and Macduff slowly brought their wooden swords together, the audience began to laugh. Sensing that the scene required a bit more intensity, the two schoolboy actors attacked each other inexpertly with greater gusto – resulting in Macduff suffering a nasty gash to his forehead and real blood dripping all over the floor.

Hope of deliverance from the Polanski film was offered by the arrival of a new film version – the Michael Fassbender *Macbeth* in 2015 – but turned sour as it dawned on English teachers that the new film is virtually unusable in the classroom. There are no good fights and the actors mumble incomprehensibly in thick Scottish accents, prompting students to ask for the old film instead.

Given the choice, which I haven't been, I would probably have opted for *Macbeth* rather than *Romeo and Juliet*, but the current orthodoxy dictates that we all do the same texts. Letting teachers choose which novel or play best suits them and their class, now seems to be regarded as a dangerously anarchic and outmoded way to run things, so it's *Romeo and Juliet*, again.

For a while in the 1990s and early 2000s, *Romeo and Juliet* was the Shakespeare play Year 9 (third year) pupils studied for their SATs (Standard Assessment Tests), which was how I first encountered it during Teaching Practice. I was attached to a Year 9 class for one lesson a week on Friday morning, and generally sat at the side of the room watching whilst the class read the play. Their teacher made it look very easy. After a quick recap of where they'd got to in the previous lesson, she chose volunteers for the various parts and got on with the reading, occasionally stopping to explain something they might not understand. Sadly, by the time it came round to my turn to take the lesson, they had finished reading the play. Focus had shifted, as it so often does for school pupils studying the play, to 'Who is to blame for the death of Romeo and Juliet?' Not learning my lesson from the disastrous *Lord of the Flies/Bunty* lesson the course tutor had observed, I planned a full-scale trial, involving sixteen different witnesses (it was a class of thirty-two, so each pair prepared the part for one witness), all of whom would be called to give evidence in court/at the front of the class. This involved an insane amount of preparation on an electric typewriter which belonged to my next-door neighbour in the hall of residence. Sixteen different character cards had to be written, with guidance notes and page references to help them prepare their defence or prosecution, a process which took me well into the small hours of the night before.

In the event, none of the students added a great deal to what was written on their cards and so proceedings were able to be completed within the hour and ten minutes of the lesson. The class teacher clearly thought I was mad to have gone to that amount of trouble, but was politely enthusiastic in front of the class, and the lesson ended up being a big improvement on the *Lord of the Flies* fiasco.

For a long time (until 2008 when they were scrapped almost overnight under New Labour) the SATs, pupils and teachers were told, were absolutely fundamental to the education of pupils at Key Stage 3 (Years 7–9). So important were they that schools frequently appealed against the accuracy of the external marking if they didn't like the look of their results. One year, my old school was informed of the (disastrous) marks on the final day of the summer term and insisted on lodging an appeal. Whilst staff gathered by the grass tennis courts for the traditional end-of-year barbecue, I was given the job of going through our cohort's SATs papers to find grounds for challenging the very low marks that had been awarded.

When we eventually got the result of the appeal, well into the following autumn term, we found that the marks had gone down even further. Fortunately, by that time, the students had forgotten all about them.

A neighbouring school appealed because the marking of their SATs papers was too generous, with nearly 100 per cent of their pupils achieving Level 5 or better, creating terrifying expectations for their GCSE results further down the line.

My Year 11 classes have been given a booklet containing edited highlights from the play. Down one half of each page is a translation of the text in plain English. Unfortunately, it has come out of the photocopier so faint that it is hard to read. The booklet dispenses with the rather pointless punning at the start of Act One Scene One, which is a relief. It takes some time and patience to explain how each word or phrase plays on the one before – 'coals' to 'colliers', 'colliers' to 'choler', 'choler' to 'collar', and so on – and it also means I can skirt around Sampson's unsavoury boasting, about thrusting 'maids to the wall', taking their virginity, and his 'tool'/'naked weapon'.

Instead, their booklet launches into the play from where the two sets of servants are exchanging insults – 'Do you bite your thumb' etc. Even though many teenagers devote considerable time and effort at school to insulting their peers, Shakespearian insults are, somehow, deemed to be more wholesome and educational. This section is often used by English teachers for a bit of drama because it is fairly easy to read. It also ends in a massive fight, which can help persuade boys that they want to take part, even if it is only simulated violence with their rulers ('My naked weapon is out').

As accomplished cussers themselves, I had assumed this would be right up the street of the very difficult class of Year 10 boys. In fact, they were far too busy trading insults with each other to take any notice of the text. And whether they had anything to learn from Shakespeare in this specialist area is a moot point. So quick were they to see openings for derision that it was necessary to avoid a whole catalogue of potentially incendiary words and phrases, all of which the class would have pounced on and directed to the relevant member of the class. It was even necessary to sidestep the word 'head' and related matters. 'Brain' was also a no-go area and greeted with an outbreak of what they called 'parring' (basically ridicule) aimed at the head shape of one of the boys in the class.

They also took it upon themselves to devise more sophisticated forms of the standard 'Your mum!' cuss. These included: 'Your mum's a cleaner', 'Your mum earns £4 an hour', and, eventually, 'Your mum sold her washing machine to buy your PS3' – after which the thumb biting between the Montagues and Capulets must have seemed like child's play. Having tried to isolate the worst offenders at the margins of the room, on bad days, rather tragically, the small group of quiet, well-behaved boys in the middle of the room started to look besieged by the skulduggery all around them.

In my first lesson with Year 11 last week I did my usual introduction to Shakespearian theatrical context, featuring the opening of *Hamlet* and a couple of clips from the film *Shakespeare in Love*. Encouraged by their positive attitude to the film, I showed a bit more of it in the second lesson, but quickly realised I was muddying the waters and breaking my old Head of Department's golden rule about delivering the narrative first before trying to do anything fancy. On this occasion, the coexistence of another storyline imagining how Shakespeare came to write *Romeo and Juliet* wasn't very helpful and spawned some rather confused questions. Someone on the front row even asked if the actor playing Shakespeare (Joseph Fiennes) was 'actually Shakespeare'.

On the advice of their Year Head the warring factions in one of my Year 11 classes have been put as far away from each other as possible in the seating plan. Sadly, this isn't very far away because I teach them in the smallest room in the English block, which makes social distancing of any sort something of a challenge, unless I remain glued to the whiteboard at the front of the room. It means that any aggro from break or lunch can still be carried on in whispers and gestures during the lesson when my back is turned, and sometimes when it isn't. Their enmity has found a new mode of expression as they enter the classroom and spray their hands with hand sanitiser, a white foamy substance, which twice this week has been smeared into hair and down backs.

The focus this week has been on Romeo and Juliet's behaviour when they first meet at the Capulet feast, and then during the balcony scene – the swimming pool scene in the new film. I have been trying to get the class to look past Leonardo DiCaprio and see some of the sillier aspects of Romeo's behaviour. This has included introducing them to the concept of *courtly love* and two of Shakespeare's sonnets – Sonnet 18 ('Shall I compare thee to a summer's day') and Sonnet 130 ('My mistress' eyes are nothing like the sun'), which is a curmudgeonly parody on the excesses found in standard love sonnets – exactly the sort of things Romeo comes out with in Act Two Scene Two in 'Capulet's orchard' as he looks up at Juliet on her balcony:

> Two of the fairest stars in all the heaven,
> Having some business, do entreat her eyes
> To twinkle in their spheres till they return.
> What if her eyes were there, they in her head?
> The brightness of her cheek would shame those
> stars...

To demonstrate the idea of natural images being a rather predictable formula in romantic compliments, I asked three volunteers to woo another volunteer, sat at the front of the room on the teacher's swivel chair (and so probably in contravention of COVID distancing protocols). The wooing consisted of three rounds in which the silver-tongued suitors completed lines from Sonnet 130 by inserting their own simile: 'My mistress' eyes are like _____ ', followed by 'lips' and 'hair'. When I have used this in the past, with classes of boys, I stuck to the running order of Shakespeare's sonnet, which meant that 'lips' were followed by 'breasts' – an excuse, as I recall, for lots of suggestions of outsized fruit. At least this was consistent with the nature theme. Today in round three the first offering was 'My mistress' hair is like black wires', which had the merit of being factually correct (the 'mistress' being wooed was a boy who wears his hair in braids) but did nothing for the point I was trying to make. The literal tendencies of some of the students in the class surfaced again later in the week when they demanded to know if Romeo was also a virgin. Juliet clearly thinks so, I said, but otherwise I am afraid I don't know, was all I could say.

Less confusing than courtly love is the fact that Romeo does say some very silly things during Act Two Scene Two. To Juliet's question, 'How cam'st thou hither' he replies with, 'With love's light wings did I o'erperch these walls.' Juliet continues this rather dry line of questioning with, 'By whose direction found'st thou out this place?' to which he answers, 'By Love... he lent me counsel.' A mixed class of teenage boys and girls have absolutely no problem comprehending that Juliet, a fourteen-year-old girl, is much more mature than her new boyfriend, even if he does seem to be a few years older.

There was obviously a testy response from schools to Ofqual's announcement at the start of the week about dropping the nineteenth-century novel (*A Christmas Carol* in our case) rather than the poetry. The next day, Ofqual sent schools an email saying that they were 'listening' to the views of teachers, preparing the way for another U-turn, which was confirmed shortly after. Schools will have a bit more flexibility about which unit they drop. Obviously, that won't include Shakespeare, which remains the only dish on the Year 11 menu for this half-term.

Attempted an innovation today with the more studious of my two Year 11 classes – using copies of the actual play in place of the booklet. The subject of the lesson was the Nurse, who, the last time they saw her in the film, was helping herself to a plate of sandwiches from the fridge. In order for this not to be what they mention in their exam in the event of a question on the Nurse, I decided to introduce them to some of the sillier and seedier lines missing from their edited version. Having recoiled previously from the idea of the Nurse wet nursing the infant Juliet, the class were equally unenthusiastic about her account of how Juliet was weaned, although the discussion got off to a difficult start with some of the class admitting they had mixed up weaning with circumcision. Too much embarrassing information about the Nurse's 'dugs' was the general consensus – 'For I had then laid wormwood to my dug' – and they had a point. But it is hard to talk about the Nurse without bringing sex into the conversation. This means explaining the 'wanton blood' she sees rushing into Juliet's cheeks, and what she means by 'you shall bear the burden soon at night' about Juliet's wedding night. For her second wedding night, in Act Four, she seems to be anticipating a sexual Olympics with 'The County Paris' who, she says, 'hath set up his rest that you shall rest but little. God forgive me!'

In an effort to sidestep the word sex and conscious that 'bawdy' might simply confuse matters, I settled on 'saucy' for describing the Nurse's behaviour. The problem with saying anything is that students tend to latch on to it and repeat it in their written responses, and, even from a two-metre safe distance, I could see that 'saucy' was cropping up in their work rather more than I intended.

Understandably, the class seemed happier exploring the Nurse's stupidity, like this particularly pointless exchange with Romeo:

Nurse: Doth not rosemary and Romeo begin with a letter?

Romeo: Ay, Nurse, what of that? Both with an R.

And she also makes a terrible job of looking after Juliet, following the death of Tybalt. She makes no attempt to manage Juliet's grief and conflicting emotions but just comes straight out with it: 'Ah weraday, he's dead, he's dead! We are undone, lady we are undone. Alack the day, he's gone, he's killed, he's dead!' Nor does she spare Juliet from the gory details – 'I saw the wound... All in gore blood.' Having declared it all to be the fault of men, she follows up with, 'Ah, where's my man?'

and an order for 'some aqua-vitae' – a nip of brandy to revive her spirits. A bit later, having listened to Friar Lawrence lecture Romeo for the best part of two pages, she responds with, 'O Lord, I could have stayed here all the night to hear good counsel. O, what learning is!'

Meanwhile, my first Year 11 class reached the end of the film today. It's been my main coping strategy during a week and a half of hot weather, but it means I have got through it with almost indecent haste, and at least three weeks ahead of the timings envisaged in the department's scheme of work. We only had the last fifteen minutes to watch in today's lesson, in what proved to be a catharsis-free screening of Romeo and Juliet's final moments. I was grateful that the Capulet vault is so well-lit in the Baz Luhrmann film because the picture quality on the whiteboard is so poor that any night-time or dimly-lit scenes simply appear as a black screen, at which point the class lose interest and start talking. Thankfully, they were able to see Romeo drink the 'dram of poison', to which one boy on the back row responded with, 'Fancy doing that over a girl!' No sooner had he been shushed and scolded by some of the more sensitive souls in the room, than another boy stood up, put his coat on, and announced, 'I've got my interview, sir', and left the room to talk to a member of SLT (Senior Leadership Team) about his non-response to remote learning.

It was the turn of the other Year 11 group to

finish the film today. I'd deliberately held it back for Wednesday last period, when getting them to do any work becomes much harder. Even with better sound and picture quality and slightly better behaviour and higher levels of maturity, they refused to engage emotionally with the climax of the play. The film shows Juliet coming round from Friar Lawrence's forty-two-hour sleeping potion before Romeo has even drunk the poison. 'She's literally moving!' said one girl impatiently. When Juliet fails to react quickly enough to the situation – i.e. Romeo killing himself – another girl called out, 'Don't stare, you silly cow! He's just about to kill himself!'

Even with Romeo dead and Juliet clearly about to follow him, the mood in the class remained very relaxed. 'He has nice hands,' sighed a girl on the front row. Harder to fathom was the question from the boy who sits next to her – 'Do the houses [Montague and Capulet] have different colours?' – at which point I felt it necessary to stop the film and find out what he was on about, or why he felt this was a point of interest at this moment in the play. After quite a bit of confused questioning it emerged that in the cartoon version, *Gnomeo & Juliet*, which several of them said was much better, one side wear red and the other blue. Another point of interest I hadn't anticipated are the many candles illuminating Juliet in the Capulet tomb, and in one row the girls seemed to be more concerned about the prospect of Romeo and Juliet setting themselves alight than about the poison and the pistol (instead of the knife Juliet uses in the play) that do actually finish them off.

Having watched the ending, later in the week I set about introducing both groups to what I have started calling the 'context box' – a large box drawn on the whiteboard, filled with squiggly lines, representing the mess Shakespeare makes of the social order and Christian morality; and a smaller one, representing Act Five Scene Three (the final scene), where he tidies everything up. In order to explain why this is inevitable or necessary, students are forced to refer to the contextual factors (Assessment Objective 3) on the handout provided.

Act Five Scene Three opens with Paris and Romeo and their servants. As tends to be the case in Shakespeare's tragedies, no matter how weak and foolish members of the nobility may have been up to this point, at the very end Shakespeare puts them back on top. Here our hitherto foppish lovers start behaving like strong men, giving orders and being obeyed – 'Give me thy torch, boy', 'Do as I bid thee, go', 'Give me that mattock and the wrenching iron', 'Hold, take this letter.' Romeo in his new guise may threaten to 'tear' poor Balthasar 'joint by joint' if he doesn't keep his distance, but sends him on his way with a purse full of money as a good master should.

Less helpful for the last-minute repair job on the nobility is the fact that Paris and Romeo fight, and Paris is killed – 'O, I am slain!' The solution is for Romeo to somehow not have known who he was fighting. 'Let me peruse this face,' says Romeo, but only after having killed the most eligible bachelor in Verona and a 'kinsman' of the Prince and his friend Mercutio. Instead of lying low for a bit, Romeo's father, Lord Montague, announces that he'll commemorate Juliet with a 'statue of pure gold', and Capulet will do the same for Romeo.

As well as restoring the proper social order the ending also reintroduces Christian morality. Even though he's not exactly covered himself in glory, Friar Lawrence gets to put the record straight and manages to emerge with some credit – 'We still have known thee for a holy man' – despite trying to lay the blame elsewhere. The deaths of Romeo and Paris are described, with a certain amount of bare-faced cheek, as 'this work of heaven'. His long speech also contains some judicious sucking-up to the nobility – 'noble Paris and true Romeo' – whilst Juliet is 'Romeo's faithful wife' on the strength of their four-day-old marriage.

Right at the end, in a move straight out of the final scene in an episode of *Scooby-Doo*, Balthasar pops up with a letter from Romeo to his father. 'This letter doth make good the Friar's words,' says the Prince, before asserting his right as an absolute ruler to proceed as he sees fit – 'Some shall be pardoned, and some punished' – and ending with a soothing rhyming couplet, as Shakespeare plays invariably do.

Chapter Eleven

Othello

A last-minute repair job was also required at the end of my first year of A level teaching. My Head of Department had asked me to teach *Othello* to the A level English Literature group, not realising that it was no longer on the syllabus. His error went undetected until the day of the final exam when the boys opened the exam paper and found that there were no questions on the play they had been studying all year. The exam was held up whilst my old Head of Department went off to ring the exam board for further instructions. He managed to do this without betraying the slightest note of panic or embarrassment, and the exam board very obligingly faxed through alternative questions for *Othello*, allowing him to blame the confusion on a printing error.

Happily, after a short absence, our exam board saw sense and restored *Othello* to the A level syllabus. This coincided with an excellent new film version (new in 1995) starring Laurence Fishburne as Othello and

Kenneth Branagh as Iago. This meant that it was now possible to teach *Othello* to any year group, as long as you stopped the film from time to time to explain what was happening and what the characters were talking about. This has to include an explanation of what Iago is shouting about beneath Brabantio's balcony in Act One Scene One: 'Right Year 7, can anybody tell me what Iago means by *making the beast with two backs*?' There is general delight once the extent of his rudeness is exposed, and with one class of Year 10 boys, 'an old black ram is tupping your white ewe' quickly became the much quoted answer to every question.

The new film also meant a release for English teachers from the old Laurence Olivier film, with its dodgy *Jackanory Playhouse* sets and even dodgier message for black people: the National Theatre of Great Britain would rather cast a famous white man for the role, and then blacken his face and lower his voice, than give the part to a black actor. Conversely, having the part played by Laurence Fishburne, instantly recognisable for a while as Morpheus from *The Matrix* films, gave *Othello* extra street credibility and a definite advantage over other Shakespeare plays.

Another advantage of teaching *Othello* is that it has also been excellent preparation for teaching *Romeo and Juliet*, basically because it contains a lot of the same ingredients: foolish, love-struck/silver-tongued nobles, an even saltier and foul-mouthed servant than any that work for the Capulets or Montagues, more sensible female victims, more blustering and ineffectual male leaders – all of which requires another rather cheesy tidy-up in the final scene.

The Romeo role in *Othello* is shared between two characters – Roderigo, the foolish young nobleman in love with Desdemona, and Cassio, Othello's smooth lieutenant, who has all the romantic talk. At the start of Act Two, Cassio does his best to proclaim Desdemona's beauty to the locals waiting for her and Othello to arrive in Cyprus. Having concluded that she is 'One that excels the quirks of blazoning pens' he immediately sets about trying to prove himself wrong with his nonsensical speech about the 'guttered rocks and congregated sands' on the seabed. In a storm, these would normally, Cassio argues, 'clog the guiltless keel' and slow the ship down. But on this occasion – 'having sense of (Desdemona's) beauty' – they back off 'letting go safely by the divine Desdemona'. And when she does arrive, as a result of this ahead of schedule, it is Cassio who leads the cheerleading: 'O, behold, the riches of the ship is come on shore! You men of Cyprus, let her have your knees.'

Desdemona has to put up with quite a lot of this sort of thing during her short stay in Cyprus. Some of it comes from Othello himself, who greets her in Act Two as his 'fair warrior' and invites the winds to 'blow till they have wakened death', providing Desdemona is waiting for him at the harbour. But for his wedding night, he slips back into the no-nonsense voice of the professional soldier: 'Come, my dear love, the purchase made, the fruits are to ensue; that profit's yet to come 'tween me and you.'

When we next see Othello, quelling a drunken brawl started by his officer Cassio, his primary concern is that his 'gentle love' has been woken up. 'All's well now, sweeting,' he assures her, and 'come away to bed', and so begins his wrapping of her in cotton wool, something she clearly starts to resent. Cassio is stripped of his position for fighting/waking Desdemona up and, prompted by Iago, turns to her for help. Having agreed to take on Cassio's case amid a flurry of legal jargon ('warrant', 'article', 'solicitor'), Desdemona sets about persuading Othello to reinstate him as his lieutenant, but is palmed-off with, 'Not now, sweet Desdemon.' This earns Othello a stiff talking-to, but he still can't help himself and tells her, 'I will deny thee nothing.' Iago understands this all too well, and is the only one of the male characters who manages to treat Desdemona like a human being. As he says to Roderigo: 'The wine she drinks is made of grapes.' And like the boy in my Year 11 class studying *Romeo and Juliet*, he also rules out doing anything rash over 'the love of a guinea-hen'. He would rather, he says, 'change my humanity with a baboon'.

Not that he is entirely indifferent to Desdemona,

but loves her, he explains, 'Not out of absolute lust.' Of greater concern for Iago is that he suspects 'the lusty Moor', and also Cassio, of sleeping with his wife Emilia – 'with my night-cap', as he puts it. This seems highly unlikely, but there's not much love lost between husband and wife. He calls her 'a foolish wife' and she seems to have given up on him, even handing over Desdemona's special handkerchief, just 'to please his fantasy'.

Despite his taste for bombast and long speeches, and it being Othello's name in the title, Iago has almost 300 lines more than his master, and it is essential that whoever's reading the part is up to the job. Vaingloriously, I have often given myself the part of Othello, and tried by this means to drag the class reading along at a good pace. Hopefully, my reading has improved since I was in the sixth form, when we studied the two Roman plays for our A level – *Julius Caesar* and *Antony and Cleopatra*. During the course of one particular school day I was given, in successive English lessons, the part of Brutus and then Mark Antony – what we called 'doing an Anthony Quayle', a famous Shakespearian actor, and the voice of both Brutus and Mark Antony on the long-playing records of the plays that our teacher would put on when he'd had enough of listening to us try to read. A quarter of an hour into the second lesson, during a stretch of *Antony and Cleopatra* where Mark Antony is doing most of the talking, I realised that the rest of the class were doing the 'wind it up' gesture. Then one of my friends broke ranks and suggested I try putting some expression into it – a totally new concept for my seventeen-year-old self to have to take on board.

Fortunately, the Roman plays and Anthony Quayle weren't part of the RSC's summer season that our English teachers took us to in Stratford-upon-Avon in 1984. There were no seats or seat belts in the school minibus then – we just sat in the back facing each other on the benches along each side of the bus. We had never seen our English teacher, Mr Tooth, drive before, and there were some comments from the back along the lines of 'Where's your bicycle, sir?' his preferred means of transport. Somewhere in the middle of England Mr Tooth approached a roundabout far too quickly and crashed into the back of a black Mercedes-Benz with a diplomatic number plate. In fact, the minibus came off worse because, to avoid hitting the Mercedes full-on, he had turned into a raised concrete barrier and badly damaged the suspension. Our group had to sit in a field for three hours waiting to be picked up by a hire bus, and only just made it in time to see Antony Sher scooting around on crutches for his Richard III.

A few weeks later, by which time the minibus had been repaired, Mr Tooth missed our double lesson on Friday afternoon because the Headmaster – who'd obviously never seen him drive – made him catch the train to somewhere in Warwickshire so that he could drive the minibus back himself, a 'punishment' as Iago says, 'more in policy than in malice', and a way of sending out a message to unruly PE teachers who regarded the vehicle as their own property and drove like madmen. Unlike Cassio, who loses his job after his moment of madness – the drunken fight in Act Two – Mr Tooth was back at school the following week, with his job and reputation intact; in fact, possibly enhanced given that we regarded him as a gentle soul, really far too undemonstrative to be put in charge of anything bigger than a bicycle.

For Othello, who lives life at full throttle, being stopped in his tracks hits him much harder. The mere suspicion that Desdemona and Cassio are secret lovers inspires another long speech devoted, somewhat confusingly, almost entirely to the military – 'Farewell the plumed troops and the big wars... Farewell the neighing steed...' – and ends with him concluding 'Farewell! Othello's occupation's gone.' Othello has clearly never heard of burying yourself and your troubles in your work, but Iago has got him into such a state that he's not thinking straight: 'By the world, I think my wife be honest, and think that she is not; I think that thou [Iago] art just, and think thou art not.' This is a far cry from earlier in Act Three Scene Three where he offers to be exchanged 'for a goat' in the unlikely event that he gives in to jealousy: 'No, Iago,

I'll see before I doubt; when I doubt prove; and on the proof, there is no more but this: away at once with love or jealousy!'

This is all very well in theory but is much more difficult and painful for him in practice. In the absence of any evidence, Othello is dangling by a thread, desperate for some sort of certainty, until Iago tells him an unlikely story about Cassio spilling the beans in his sleep – 'there are a kind of men so loose of soul that in their sleeps will mutter their affairs' – and then, for good measure, says that he saw Cassio 'wipe his beard' with Desdemona's special handkerchief. This does the trick as far as Iago is concerned, although why he's going to all this trouble to destroy everyone else's happiness is never properly explained. But on the strength of this flimsy evidence Othello has his certainty – 'I'll tear her to pieces!' – and Iago can afford to start enjoying himself, mischievously throwing in a plea for 'Patience, I say: your mind perhaps may change.' Iago already knows the answer ('Never, Iago') but, even with Othello's tendency to go round the houses, may not have expected his reply would take in the Black Sea ('Pontic sea'), the Sea of Marmora ('Propontic') and the Dardanelles ('Hellespont').

There is no going back and Act Five brings matters to a head, with Iago setting Roderigo on to murder Cassio, and Othello planning the same for Desdemona. The slow and painful countdown to Desdemona's death in Act Five Scene Two begins in Act Five Scene One with a brief cameo/advertisement from Othello, presumably from up on the balcony: 'Strumpet, I come!'

Down below Roderigo has botched the killing of Cassio and been wounded – prematurely announcing 'I am slain!' – and Cassio also fears the worst after receiving a stab to the leg from Iago: 'I am maimed for ever.' In fact, Cassio lives and Roderigo has to be finished off by Iago a couple of pages later. The melodramatic descriptions of their injuries, plus the many references to needing a light, and the general simulation of confusion and darkness, make this an excellent scene for demonstrating the impact of theatrical context on Shakespeare's writing.

Some years ago, I had reached this point in the play with the upper sixth A level group when Ofsted descended. At the time, Ofsted, we were told, wanted to see active learning. Teachers needed to zip it and let their pupils do the talking, so a bit of drama/melodrama involving Act Five Scene One seemed just the thing for my double lesson in periods one and two.

It's fair to say that this particular group weren't quite so bothered about the inspection as their teachers and five minutes after the bell had sounded for the start of the lesson only one of them had shown up. I looked at the inspector as if to say what do you want me to do. The show, he indicated, had to go on, but he then got up and left with a shake of the head and Arnold Schwarzenegger's line from *The Terminator*, 'I'll be back.' The other members of the class then arrived at five-minute intervals for the first twenty-five minutes of the lesson. Not quite the clean start I was looking for, or learning beginning immediately, but no matter as the inspector wasn't there.

He didn't return until well into the second period, by which time we'd done all the interesting or active things I'd planned. 'Don't worry, sir,' one of the boys said when I explained my predicament. 'We'll just do it again when he comes in.'

And, despite having had a dry run half an hour earlier, the group's re-enactment of the action at the start of Act Five Scene One was so chaotic and unprofessional that the inspector had no reason to suspect anything.

After the quick burst of chaotic action in Act Five Scene One, the pace slows a little for the final scene. Despite his earlier remark that 'when I love thee not, chaos is come again', Othello manages to open with a soliloquy nearly in perfect iambic pentameter, which is one of several puzzling contradictions in what follows. Desdemona, after a desperate struggle, is suffocated with her pillow, but still has enough breath to say goodbye to Emilia two pages later, and take the rap for her own death:

Emilia: O, who hath done this deed?
Des: Nobody – I myself – farewell.
          Commend me to my kind Lord – O,
          farewell!

Even so, Emilia clearly suspects foul play and turns on Othello in surprisingly biblical language, suggestive of a sudden conversion to Christianity. At the end of Act Four Emilia had stoutly defended her right to a little 'sweet and sour' on the side – 'who would not make her husband a cuckold... I should venture purgatory for't' – but two scenes later can't comprehend her mistress being 'false to wedlock'. And having kept quiet about the stolen handkerchief, despite witnessing Othello raging over its loss, she now scolds Iago for telling 'a lie, an odious damned lie. Upon my soul, a lie, a wicked lie!'

Iago now has nowhere to hide, but kills Emilia, his wife, for good measure and makes a run for it, hotly pursued by Montano. This leaves Gratiano – Desdemona's uncle, and presumably a relatively senior citizen – to guard 'Valiant Othello', the great warrior. Fortunately for Gratiano, Othello is too busy beating himself up to take advantage of the mismatch: 'Blow me about in winds! Roast me in sulphur! Wash me in steep-down gulfs of liquid fire! O Desdemona!'

It is essential that lowly Iago, who has been running the show up to this point, is put in his place, and that the nobility he's been running rings round regain some credibility. Iago is, therefore, quickly apprehended and referred to from this point as a 'damned slave', and, despite his previous criminal genius, is suddenly made to look like an amateur, with his plan discovered, spelt out in letters they find in Roderigo's pocket. Like Emilia, Cassio also discovers God at the end of the play, and conveniently sidesteps his own whoring and drunken brawling to condemn Iago as 'Most heathenish and most gross!' Despite previously having looked incapable of being in charge of anything, Cassio is elevated to 'Lord Governor' and now 'rules in Cyprus'.

Before the curtain is brought down with another soothing rhyming couplet, from Lodovico, the voice of the Venetian establishment, Othello gets to say 'a word or two' himself. Regular iambic pentameter won't do for this and as Othello reaches full poetic lift-off the lines crash through the ten-syllable speed limit for the beautiful climax:

> Then must you speak
> Of one that loved not wisely, but too well;
> Of one, not easily jealous but, being wrought,
> Perplexed in the extreme; of one whose hand
> Like the base Indian threw a pearl away
> Richer than all his tribe; of one whose subdued
> eyes,
> Albeit unused to the melting mood,

Drop tears as fast as the Arabian trees
Their medicinable gum.

After a quick reminder that this 'extravagant and wheeling stranger' has aligned himself with Europe and Christianity, 'He stabs himself.'

Pupils are genuinely moved by the events at the end of the play. The film is always watched in hushed silence, and then to cover their embarrassment at their emotional reaction, someone will say, 'Good film that, sir' and normal conversation resumes.

Chapter Twelve

Postscript

After a three-week furlough doing something else, Year 10 are back on *Lord of the Flies*. Despite complaining bitterly that they spent most of last year studying it, I suspect most of them neglected Piggy and Ralph during lockdown. Their responses suggest widely varying degrees of knowledge and most of the class have probably forgotten much of what they did know. They are, however, uniformly unenthusiastic, and starting to resort to a kind of shared gallows humour. Yesterday, when I put the old black and white film on, I heard someone ask if anyone had any rope. They regard the film with incredulity – no colour, no soundtrack, no HD picture quality, no real actors – but it doesn't stop them asking for it every time they arrive for a lesson. It's better, they've realised, than reading the book, or doing work.

Reading the book hasn't gone very smoothly so far. On this occasion, this has had nothing to do with Golding's dense prose and lame dialogue, but is down to the copies of the text I've inherited. Different versions of a text, with different page numbers, always leads to confusion and an endless stream of 'What page, sir?' To avoid this in their next lesson I just gave out the version which matched my copy, which meant some of them had to share. Any hope that we'd all be on the same page quickly vanished when – with evident delight – they started reporting missing pages. Ignoring my plea for them to just do their best, a number of them laid out the loose pages on their desk in rows, as if playing Patience, and then failed to put them back in the correct order, judging from the moaning and groaning of the other Year 10 group that followed them.

The not very well-bound Faber & Faber edition says, 'Winner of the Nobel Prize for Literature' on the front cover, prompting one boy to call out, 'How did this win a prize?' 'The reason is simple,' according to the Nobel Committee, 'These [Golding's] books are very entertaining and exciting', something I decided not to share with them. Fortunately, the English Department has also produced a booklet for *Lord of the Flies*, containing the key extracts (but sadly not page numbers). Last week – hoping for a more streamline lesson – I put the five short extracts the class were going to be looking at on a double-sided handout, the first three on one side and the other two on the back. They were also numbered 1–5 and projected on to the whiteboard.

'I haven't got that, sir!' complained a boy on the front row as soon as I began.

This wasn't quite true. He had somehow failed to locate the first extract, all the way over on the other side of the handout.

Post-COVID, officially, we are not supposed to lose our temper and vent our spleen at difficult pupils, for fear that droplets of saliva will be sent flying all over pupils in the front row. On this occasion, however, I couldn't help myself.

The boy sat there looking unperturbed and when I had finished it was left to his neighbour to turn the sheet over for him.

Last week, when as many as ten pupils were missing from each of my Year 10 lessons, I did start to wonder if we were heading for a gloomy recreation of the novel's 'survival of the fittest' theme. In a total reversal of schools' usual emphasis on resilience, students have been told to stay at home if they have so much as a runny nose and the sniffles. However, this seems to have been a blip and most of them are back this week.

It's early days, but so far they've shown rather less solidarity with their state school comrade, Piggy, than the girls at the posh independent school. The only emotional involvement I have detected so far has been with the real pigs on the island, the first of which was butchered in the film at the end of today's lesson. 'That's disgusting!' was the general reaction, not just to the killing itself, but also to the rudimentary cooking and eating with greasy fingers that followed. One girl ignored my advice about not taking anything in *Lord of the Flies* too literally, and wanted to know if the boys in the film actually killed the pig. In a previous lesson, when I had suggested that Piggy's name didn't just reflect his physique but also the superior intelligence he shares with pigs, she wasn't having any of it.

'What are you talking about, sir? Pigs like rolling in mud. How are they clever?'

At the end of the lesson, as the class were packing up their things, another girl asked me, very politely, but with an unmistakably plaintive and weary air, what they would be studying next after half-term. I could hardly bring myself to form the answer, which is *A Christmas Carol*. Either side of Remembrance Sunday would be the ideal time to read *Journey's End*, and was in happier times. But this year, it has just occurred to me, after half-term I am supposed to be teaching *A Christmas Carol* for sixteen of my twenty-one lessons in the school week – revision with my two Year 11 classes and starting it from scratch with Year 10. There's really no getting out of it, unless I do a Hibbert, the flaky officer in *Journey's End*, who tries to get sent home with neuralgia. When this doesn't work he invites his superior officer, Stanhope, to put him out of his misery permanently: 'I swear I'll never go into those trenches again. Shoot! – and thank God.'

I could just teach something else and hope nobody notices. For teachers there are some advantages as a result of the coronavirus and social distancing: schools are happy for you to share a room with thirty pupils but much more squeamish about adults sharing the same spaces, which means there are currently no lesson observations, no learning walks, no full Ofsted inspections, and also no Teaching Assistants in your lessons, who might grass you up to the Head of Department if you went off-piste. So it might be worth checking in the stock cupboard to see if there is a class set – or four – of *Pride and Prejudice*. It's still on the syllabus, I think.

Also by Simon Pickering

THOSE WHO CAN'T... A TEACHER'S GAP YEARS

Green
Publications

In and out of post-communist Poland

Chapter One

Leicester – Toruń / Waldek / Shopping / Mercy
Schwimmer / The Ruffs

In March 1990 I finally received two offers of permanent employment. Blockbuster Video were opening a big new store on London Road and the manager, Mike, was quick to offer me a job.

'I need you here early Saturday morning. There's going to be builders and all sorts of shite crawling round here. I want you to hold the fort till I get here. Good lad.'

Mike didn't pretend to be interested in my post-graduate research and conducted the informal interview on his terms. 'If Robson (the Managing Director) says he wants those boxes shifted I'll do it myself. I don't mind getting covered in crap if I am taking home thirty K. You did a degree – fair play to you – but what are you earning now?'

There was no post-graduate research but I needed a cover story to explain my sudden conversion to 'retail' and 'the product' (videos). I also felt it necessary to show Mike that I was in it for the long haul, and so described my 'research' as 'a slow boat to China', as if he cared.

In fact I managed only six weeks. This was more than Assistant Managers Rob and Graham, sacked after only a few weeks in a ruthless cull, and more than I had expected after a rowdy Saturday night visit from some friends loudly asking for 'that film Bumfuckers'. I promised Mike it would never happen again and was given a second chance.

There was also an offer from a Professor Pawlik to teach in the Department of English Philology at Nicolaus Copernicus University in Toruń, Poland. I met his envoy, Mr Krzeszewski, on the fourteenth floor of the Humanities building at the University. A thin man wearing a bobble hat and large glasses stepped out of the paternoster.

There was something rather goofy about him, which – despite his heavy accent and serious manner – quickly put me at my ease. It also helped that none of the other post-graduate students (post post-graduate in my case) to whom the job had been advertised had applied. Mr Krzeszewski kept his bobble hat on throughout our meeting. Basically the job was mine if I wanted it.

Neither appointment impressed my two housemates. Alan, contemplating a move to London and an investment in sun bed rental, was particularly critical. 'Poland! Fucking hell mate. What do you want to go to Poland for? You're better off sticking at Blockbusters.' Alistair joined in but at least promised to visit.

Mr Krzeszewski was there to meet me at the railway station when I arrived in Toruń towards the end of September. We squeezed ourselves uncomfortably into his tiny Fiat, whilst my luggage followed on behind in a taxi, and drove to the flat provided for me by the university.

At no stage had it been a comfortable journey. In Dover I had been cheerfully informed of a rail strike disrupting trains out of Ostend. This was to be miraculously lifted minutes before the departure of my train to Warsaw, but the prospect of an unscheduled stay in Belgium had done nothing to brighten the three-hour crossing. I settled down in my compartment in the company of an Austrian Mormon and an Irishman who kept repeating 'Yes' to himself every few seconds. He was on his way to see the Berlin wall before it was pulled down but constantly fretted about being on the wrong train. In the end he and the Austrian got off the train somewhere in Belgium. Otherwise there seemed to be virtually nobody on the train until we stopped in Berlin early the following morning, when the compartment – which I had come to regard as my own – filled with suspicious looking strangers.

At the Polish border soldiers boarded the train demanding passports and visas. I had no visa only a typed letter from the university. The first soldier muttered something about a 'problem' and disappeared with my passport. Other soldiers passed through the train double-checking everyone's papers but this time I couldn't even produce my passport. I expected at any moment to be led off of the train in disgrace. Eventually the soldiers returned with a hurriedly issued visa and a bill for 442,000 złoty! They agreed to take sterling and I prepared to part with all of my hard currency. In fact, the train was held in the station whilst the soldier went off to check the exchange rate, returning a few minutes later with a bill for £26. Was this an act of clemency, I wondered. Perhaps it was merely a down payment and the visa proper would have to be applied for later on arrival. I was delighted, therefore, when the soldier re-appeared with my change – 68,000 złoty (or £4).

The train finally got going again and I returned to my compartment to cold stares all round. Outside the landscape seemed to become more and more dismal: flat scrubby plains – perfect for a tank battle – interspersed with heavy tracts of forest; there were no friendly hedgerows, just vast unkempt grassland. All I had seen of Poland previously were the dark snow covered streets behind the BBC correspondent Tim Sebastian, from his reports during martial law, and also footage of the Gdańsk shipyard during the

Solidarity strike – pictures of men with checked shirts and moustaches sleeping inside the shipyard buildings. I had been expecting heavy industry and blocks of grim apartments not open country with an occasional farmer toiling behind a horse and plough.

Towards midday we stopped in a desolate looking siding. Passengers got out and smoked and local men moved through the compartments selling bottles of beer from old sports bags. Had I known it, my change for the visa could have bought the entire contents of one well-stocked bag.

A couple of hours later, in Poznań, I boarded an even slower train which took me the rest of the way to Toruń.

'So we will go now, erm, to your neighbour Waldek Skrzypek,' Mr Krzeszewski said as we arrived at my flat. He might have added 'who lives next door', but instead left me to contemplate folding myself back into his Fiat.

By the time I arrived in Toruń, Professor Pawlik had left for America and a visiting professorship. He had, it appeared, still found time to arrange my reception; I was to put myself entirely in the hands of Waldek, to whose apartment and warm welcome I was delivered that first evening.

'Ahhhh. Mr Adam! Let me look at you. Please come in. Yes, please sit here.'

Waldek ushered me to the leather chair in which he placed all visitors and then disappeared, returning shortly after with a tray of snacks and a bottle of vodka.

After a few pleasantries – I was invited for tea the following day – Mr Krzeszewski made his excuses and left. Waldek, with his black linen suit and cigarettes seemed terribly cosmopolitan by comparison and was, I imagined, an East European intellectual, albeit one playing Chris Rea's Greatest Hits.

Waldek shared his small flat with his wife Basia and their precociously musical daughter Emilia, but had made the living room his own. Instead of the usual 70s' wall unit, Waldek housed his books on cognitive linguistics in an elegant teak bureau. An almost antique typewriter sat on the leather-covered desktop and there was a piano and a classical guitar.

This didn't seem to be the time to ask what was really on my mind. 'But what am I to teach them?' asks the timid hero of Evelyn Waugh's novel *Decline and Fall*. My teaching experience up to this point consisted of two weeks teaching English to a small group of Austrian boys who were attending a residential school during the Easter holidays. During the dark days at Blockbuster Video I had dutifully applied to do a PGCE (Post Graduate Certificate of Education). My first choice had been Leicester University's School of Education, but after an extremely short interview I had received a letter of rejection. In fact the course tutor terminated my interview after two minutes, after I had admitted, rather unwisely, that I didn't actually want to be a teacher but that I needed 'something lined up for next year'. Instead of dressing smartly I had worn jeans and the customised donkey jacket I wore for all other occasions. For my second interview at Nottingham University I swapped this for a suit and tie and tried to say all the right things. It worked and they even let me put off doing the course for a year so that I could go to Poland.

Waldek, however, had just returned from an academic conference at Keele University, and spoke expansively of his PhD research; he was clearly not the person to whom I should reveal my anxiety. (In fact the answer from Captain Grimes – 'Oh, I shouldn't try to teach them anything, not just yet anyway.' – was closer to Waldek's relaxed work ethic than I could have appreciated.)

For now though, I was reluctant to part with my man-of-the-world status – implicit I liked to think in the bottle of vodka – and so drank my share as if pickled cucumbers and bison grass vodka were all standard procedure.

The next morning I was woken by the rattle of the trams passing in the street below. Soon after Waldek arrived to take me to the university. First to the rectorate building on the main campus where I was to be processed as a university employee and then to the Collegium Maius in the old town where I would be teaching. Among the introductions was an encounter with the keeper of the photocopier – situated in a kind of prison cell deep in the basement. He seemed rather put out that I wasn't German but continued to speak German to me anyway. He persisted on my subsequent visits and I invariably came away with the wrong pages and the sound of him tutting loudly in his chair.

The Collegium Maius was a huge dark building on four floors. The English Department was situated on the third floor and by the time we reached it Waldek was breathing heavily and perspiring in his thick leather coat. The start of term was still more than two weeks away and the building was almost completely empty and yet Professor Pawlik had insisted on my early arrival. Having thrown over my oldest friend's wedding to be there on time I was somewhat dismayed to discover that not only was the Professor missing but that the rest of the department were still enjoying their holidays. The other British native speaker joining the department would also not be arriving for another week, Waldek informed me over a pizza in the Old Town – a Mr Ruff and his wife. This evoked a succession of homely images – being invited to have my tea with the older couple, kindly Mrs Ruff bringing out an apple crumble for pudding – and I immediately suggested that I should accompany Waldek when he went to meet them the following week.

Until then, however, I continued to monopolise Waldek's sitting room. When I visited him that evening he was in high spirits. Basia was out at work and there was a gleam in his eye as he reappeared carrying a bottle of vodka on a silver tray. It was still light outside and a warm breeze blew in through the open door to the balcony. Waldek put on a Chris Rea tape and sat back with a sigh of contentment.

'Ah Adam! While the cat's away... cheers! Let me bring you something to eat. Some cheese? Some sausage perhaps?'

When he returned from the kitchen Waldek attempted to explain his PhD thesis. It would have to be completed within the next couple of years or there might be problems remaining in the flat – technically in the gift of the university. Through the haze of vodka I pretended to follow what he was saying. What was cognition, I wondered?

As the evening wore on Waldek grew more sentimental. 'You know, Adam, you will find things in Poland very different to what you are used to. Everything here must seem very grey to you. All of the buildings are dirty and peeling, but for me it's beautiful. Poland is a poor country but it has wonderful forests and lakes. On Saturday you must come with us to the forest to pick mushrooms.'

This was a more significant invitation than I at first appreciated. Before going to Poland someone had told me, rather dismissively, that beetroot was the national dish. Mushrooms, in all their infinite varieties, were in fact the real source of pride amongst Poles and superior laughter greeted anyone who dared to ask the Polish word for mushrooms. 'You mean pieczarki. But we have so many other varieties of mushroom here in Poland.' Real mushrooms, it seemed, only grew wild in the forest.

Even urban Poles, who otherwise showed no affinity with the countryside, claimed intimate knowledge of the fungi growing in Polish forests. Being able to tell which were edible and which were not seemed to be a matter of national pride – a proof of their Polishness. There is even a mushroom picking scene in Poland's national epic poem, 'Pan Tadeusz' (or to give it its full title in English, 'Sir Thaddeus or the Last Lithuanian Forray: A Nobleman's Tale from the Years of 1811 and 1812 in Twelve Books of Verse'). This appears in 'Book Three: Flirtations', in which there is clearly more to mushrooms than just fungus:

> Mushrooms abounded – round the fair damsels the young men did throng;
> Or vixens, as they're hailed in Lithuanian song.
> They symbolise maidenhood, their flesh no maggot bites...

At the weekend, as he had promised, we drove out to a dark pine forest. It was damp and pleasantly spongy underfoot and whilst Basia and Emilia collected mushrooms Waldek and I stood around chatting.

'Professor Pawlik is a very clever man, Adam. He has his own way of making sure things are done. He can be very formal but really I like him. Waldemar, he will say, can I leave you to make the arrangements for the native speakers. He has a lot of influence with the Rector of the University so I am always happy to help him.'

Although I was soon to become a fan of all things Polish, I was initially deeply suspicious of everything. I avoided all dairy products and only shopped at Edward Śmigielski's, a mini western-style supermarket about the size of an average SPAR shop, where I paid hugely inflated prices for imported food products from West Germany. My first purchase was a large and very expensive tin of dried milk, a necessary alternative to the local bottled milk with its head of curdled cream. A more refined product was sold in infuriatingly floppy plastic bags, most of which ended up on the floor or in the fridge.

I didn't attempt to make a phone call or use my washing machine and shunned the tramline which ran outside my apartment block. I had located the British Council Library, however, and spent much of the first fortnight reading British campus novels in between snacks of packet soups and cheese sandwiches.

I soon realised I would not be able to shop exclusively

at Smigielski's. The advantage of shopping there, as in Tesco or Sainsbury's, was that one wasn't required to speak. Customers were trusted to pick items from the shelves themselves and enjoyed the freedom of walking around with them in a basket before paying. The alternative to exorbitant prices and decadent western practices was the traditional sklep. In the communist spirit of queuing/jobs for the girls, a sklep involved visiting/ queuing at three or four different counters and communicating with three or four different depressed shop assistants. The anonymous packaging – thick brown paper for most items not in a tin or the fridge – didn't help either, making it impossible for the silent shopper to distinguish sugar from flour, lentils from eggs etc.

An alternative to packet soup and sandwiches were the university stołówkas. These were the several canteens which catered for anyone connected or who had ever been connected with the university. Waldek had seen to it that I was given a book of tickets. This entitled me to a three course lunch in what, until the students returned, resembled a pensioners' club. There was generally pale, unpalatable soup and a main course of fried meat accompanied by cabbage and grated carrot. In case anyone should think of stealing the cutlery the point of each knife had been removed.

About the Author

What Page, Sir? is Simon Pickering's fifth book. He began writing in 2016 as a form of therapy, on the train home from his job as a school teacher – an antidote to difficult teenagers and pointless government and Senior Leadership initiatives. These are both explored in *Ambassadors and Zombies – A Teacher's Guide to Schools and Teaching*. As Adam Tangent, his alter ego, he has published *Those Who Can't – A Teacher's Gap Years*, based on his two years pretending to be a university lecturer in post-communist Poland at the start of the 1990s. In the last year he has also published *Living With Jos Buttler – six weeks in English cricket's summer of love* and *Gaza On My Mind – conversations with my brother-in-law and other Gazans*. Simon is still a school teacher and lives in Hertford with his wife and two children.

Find out more about RedDoor
Press and sign up to our
newsletter to hear about our
latest releases, author events,
exciting **competitions**
and more at

reddoorpress.co.uk

YOU CAN ALSO FOLLOW US:

 @RedDoorBooks

 Facebook.com/RedDoorPress

 @RedDoorBooks